Tony LOCORRIERE

BITCOIN SUPERSTAR

What are bitcoins?

How to make a real difference

and how to handle cryptocurrencies.

Title

BITCOIN SUPERSTAR

Author

Tony LOCORRIERE

To stay up to date:

Author Profile on Amazon

Tony LOCORRIERE

Web

https://www.tonylocorriere.org

(Where you will find a lot of free content)

Facebook

www.facebook.com/bitcoinsuperstar

(Bitcoin and Crypto Report every Saturday morning)

DISCLAIMER

This work is a literary property with all rights reserved by the author, according to law. It is expressly forbidden to reproduce even partially, especially for profit, without prior written permission. The notions contained herein are the result of years of experience, so it is not guaranteed that the same results will be achieved. The reader is aware of the risks and assumes full responsibility for their choices derived from my strategies, which are shared solely for information and educational purposes and do not represent investment advice.

COPYRIGHT

ACKNOWLEDGMENTS

First and foremost, I am particularly grateful to all those extraordinary people who over the years have helped me to shape the idea of continuous improvement, not just financial but above all human, personal and social: my mentors.

I would like to express my gratitude to all those people who, in March 2017, allowed me to be awarded the title of **Amazon Bestseller** author in the record time of twenty minutes since its launch, thanks to my previous publication. I would also like to amicably shake your hand because you have decided to undertake this demanding reading, the result of my experience in the cryptocurrency community. The great satisfaction that will reward the effort I put into the challenging writing of these pages is the possible achievement of financial well being, for you and your loved ones!

All that remains is for me to wish you pleasant and fruitful reading, in the words of one of my favourite writers, the Prince of Marsillac, François de La Rochefoucauld:

*"The mediocre mind commonly condemns
all that is beyond their reach".*

SOMMARIO

PREFACE

I have never thought I would one day find myself completely immersed in the greatest economic revolution like the one we are currently experiencing thanks to the spread of cryptocurrencies.

I assume that even the imaginary creator of the Bitcoin protocol, alias Satoshi Nakamoto, could ever have thought that a few years after the fateful 2008 he could have received such a response to his project aimed at ridiculing the traditional banking system and the debt system which it is based on. A digital currency has been created which, unlike our Euro or other currencies, sees its own buying power increase constantly. It is a currency with a definite number of already determined "pieces", to avoid the inflationary guillotine. A new currency that does not feel the need for intrinsic cash injections, on the Quantitative Easing model operated by the Central Banks of the World. Let's look around! We immediately note that the crypto currencies have fully embraced the current human phenomenon of rebellion and opposition to political, financial and sociological regimes. We are part of those generations now exasperated by everything, which determined the unexpected "Brexit" that is the exit from the Euro of Great Britain, the unexpected rise to power of Trump in the United States and the adoption of bitcoin to revolutionize the dissatisfaction with banks and the international financial system, which I call **"cryptanarchy"**! This tremendous technological and financial innovation is the cause of clashes with government institutions in many corners of the world. It could be a massive insurrection phenomenon to subvert the system, but I think it is an unprecedented speculative example of a few powerful institutions attempting to enrich the infamous, leaving behind the many unconscious small savers.

One of the most effective words in the financial field is: **trust**! Investments are made because you are confident in the future of a company, in a performing financial instrument, or in an effective manager. Cryptocurrencies (I like to call them that, and abbreviate with "**Cryptos**") are also supported by the same magical word. They are digital currencies, ruled by no one, they have no underlying foundation and they are not sustained by anything, only by the trust of those who have invested in them. Finally, we are also confident that this phenomenon can become widespread and very effective for all players, including you, when you started trusting me by ordering this book.

To further thank you, I have reserved access to my personal channels for so many new updates in various areas of interest so that you can benefit from a full pathway towards personal satisfaction!

"One of the most effective words
*in the financial field is: **trust**!"*

INTRODUCTION

It was a Saturday afternoon in December 2010. I found myself in Rome, inside a beautiful nineteenth-century room for a business presentation. Through mutual friends I was introduced to Andrea, a young man who, from the very beginning, struck me as being intelligent. Speaking to me, he told me that he had just graduated in finance and how his thesis was something like "The Developments of the Bitcoin Protocol"! Accompanying my atavistic curiosity and hunger for knowledge, I asked him what it was, apologising for my ignorance in the matter, and he told me about this phenomenon with the limited amount of data that was then available. Sincerely, I was not blown away! At the end of the brief conversation, he advised me to buy the equivalent of just €1,000 in bitcoins that at that time equated to around 5 cents a dollar. I could have bought about 20,000 pieces. We said, "Goodbye" and lost sight of each other, immersed in the hustle and bustle of the presentation. This was the greatest regret of my life, because I did not follow Andrea's advice and after about six years from that meeting, if I had invested I would have found myself with a capital of about **a few tens of millions of dollars**. Even now, if I think about it I kick myself, but you know that opportunities must always be seized at the right time, with no possible future regrets. This was one of the biggest life lessons I had to deal with. I did not hear from Andrea again, probably because he is enjoying his fortune at the pool, in his mega villa in one of the tax havens. Lucky him!

Before we resort to the explanation of the crypto-currency phenomenon, I think it is important to make an important preamble about the concept of **Currency**. It's a means of compensation, issued by the national government and accepted by the market. Currency that is no longer produced or that which is devalued, is no longer considered as money in as much as it is no longer accepted. In the recent past, economic transactions were governed by barter, followed by "in kind agreements" (coin-commodity), then, since the middle of the 7th century BC, the metal coin was used with an intrinsic value (gold, silver, etc.) and finally paper money, to handle the increasing volume of commerce. So, when we talk about currency, it refers to typical economic functions such as a:

•Payment instrument;
•Measurement of value;
•Valuation reserve.

The primary function is that of a payment instrument, because the others are a consequence of it. It is commonly known that coinage is desired not because of its intrinsic value (now zero) but for what having it allows you to buy! Keeping in mind this important distinction, **can crypts, be defined as coins?** Of course, they can! Even though any national authority does not issue them, they perform the three typical functions very well, measuring the value of goods/ service at the exchange rate with the national currency, already being a means of payment and embodying a considerable value reserve that appreciates in time. Many think that crypts do not have a counter value, but also the Euro, the dollar and other physical currencies are not covered by anything. They are scrap paper with a price printed on both sides, effectively only worth the five cents needed to print them. States threatens the population if they do not pay taxes in a currency with a "legal tender", such as the US dollar and the Euro in Europe. States are giving an "intrinsic" value to their currency, even if, in fact, they worth nothing. By now, this state of affairs is perceived as real political abuse, and we no longer like playing this game! The debt black hole is getting bigger and bigger. Markets are **"drug addicts"**, made dependent on injections of mountains of worthless money, as the Fed and the ECB have accustomed us. Taxes and charges suffocate growth, and many nations are suffering greatly, especially those with European obligations! The largest-ever currency war is in action and the usually safe and lucrative investment in gold is steadily falling despite its well-known ease of liquidation and monetization.

On the horizon, we see the economic apocalypse and a digital catharsis called **bitcoin**, which has already exceeded the price of gold / ounce. It is the current Superstar, to which many attribute the great responsibility of bringing up the fate of world economies, even if for many it is still a completely negligible phenomenon.

Finally, I have read several inaccurate books on the subject, and I have realized that the web is nothing more than a reservoir of mostly useless information about it. Referring to what was written in my previous book, I would like to apply the three fundamental areas: - **information, training, and action** to this fervent world of cryptos. This is our true starting point: To be able to convey in writing, everything that could be of assistance to those people who would like to see the crypto world with its low risks and great potential for gain.

"Investment with the highest interest rate is:

the most effective information".

DIGITAL DICTIONARY

We soon realized that those who are interested in cryptocurrencies must immediately deal with jargon that they may not necessarily know the meaning of. Our first task will be to identify and define many of the terms you commonly find at the forefront of this topic and in the various thematic discussions, without having to go elsewhere to look them up. Let's start!

Address

A Bitcoin address is equivalent to a physical address, an email, or an IBAN/BIC. It is the only identifying information that you need to provide someone with for them to be able to pay you in bitcoin. Each address (public key) should only be used for a single transaction and for that reason; many wallets automatically change them after each transaction.

Bitcoin (BTC or XBT)

It is not only the unquestioning King of Cryptocurrencies, but it is above all an innovative encrypted technology that aims to revolutionize the world economy. By international convention, the term "Bitcoin" written with a capital B refers to the protocol and the network, while in lower case it refers to the crypto value itself (BTC). Bitcoin was born from the publication of the so-called **"Communication Protocol"**, which took place in November 2008 thanks to its enigmatic creator. We will see the peculiar characteristics that distinguish it clearly from regulated national currencies. For now, know that the Bitcoin network allows the possession and the anonymous transfer of coins and is impossible for any authority, government or criminal to block transfers or obtain bitcoin without the possession of its "keys". Bitcoin is divisible up to the eighth decimal point digit. 0.00000001 BTC is the minimum amount that can be processed in a transaction. It is called "Satoshi" in honor of the founder.

Block

Blocks are key nodes that are created to record all trading transactions that are indelibly inserted into the public and shared logs. Each block contains a timestamp, that is, a link to a previous block, to which it is connected. In fact, once recorded, data in a given block cannot be modified retrospectively without altering all subsequent blocks. Just think that that the last block ever to be generated has already been predicted and it will be no. 6,929,999, which should be created in around 2140, when the total amount of BTC in circulation will be 21 Million.

Blockchain

The chain of blocks is simply a distributed data store on thousands of PCs, which is used to keep track of the list of transactions, developed on each block. This technology makes every operation public but inviolable, even more so than those of the banks. It is typically handled by a p2p network that adheres to the validation protocol of new blocks. Blockchain are resistant to data modification and are used for open and distributed accounting, which are managed efficiently and are permanently verifiable. In 2015, large companies such as Visa, Orange, and Nasdaq invested in the platform based on this technology. Banks have not been watching; Goldman Sachs has even invested fifty million dollars in technology to try to reduce costs and intermediaries. Its future is entirely rosy because according to a forecast by the World Economic Forum, by 2025 there will be many businesses that will have adopted this protocol and will generate well over 10% of "Gross Domestic Product" worldwide thanks to the incredible peculiarities of Blockchain. It will be a slow but inexorable growth!

Confirmation

More appropriately, "confirmation of the transaction" is the operation that validates each transaction. It is also necessary as it avoids "double spending", i.e. double transactions, including fraudulent transactions, as you must wait for the appropriate confirmation. When you start trading, you will usually need a few minutes to make the confirmation or confirmations through the related block transcripts, for the final legitimacy of the transfer of value.

Cryptocurrency

It is a decentralized digital currency whose implementation is based on the principles of encryption. Like any digital currency, you can make online payments securely and anonymously worldwide, with just one click.

Digital Signature

A digital signature is a mathematical scheme that demonstrates the authenticity of a message, a digital document, or the property of something sent through an unsafe channel. A valid digital signature guarantees both the recipient and the sender integrity and authenticity of the message. In the platforms, addresses are linked to private keys like a digital signature that guarantees everything, while preserving the identity of both participants in the transaction.

Double spending

It is a mistake or a fraudulent method that occurs when you start two or more transactions from the same wallet with the same cryptocurrencies within the time frame usually expected to receive confirmation of the first transaction. Do not trust anyone who tells you that you have completed the sale unless you have received confirmation!

Dump

It is about to unload, download. The cryptocurrencies move with volatile phases, called "pump and dump" which means pumping and unloading, to multiply earnings, large investors come to an agreement to pump the market at the same time and then suddenly unload it simultaneously! This behavior fuels the greed of the small investors, who not only make the decision to enter with the hope of a quick profit, but also always do so after the larger investors have been the "Market Makers".

Encryption

It means, hidden writing. It is the branch of cryptology that originally dealt with methods to make a "coded" message, so it would not be understandable and intelligible and that unauthorized people could not read it. As part of the crypt, it makes it impossible to use other keys to operate your own wallet or to make changes in the Blockchain, thus allowing a totally secure environment from illegal hackers.

Fiat coin

Modern currency framed in the monetary system of a sovereign country, according to Modern Money Theory (MMT). In economic language, it is the unconvertible paper currency, generally accepted as a means of payment having a legal or forced legality by the issuing state, irrespective of its intrinsic value. In other words, it is a payment tool that does not fully protect your well-kept savings! This is true of all national currencies and in the crypto environment we no longer use the terms Euros, Dollars and Yen but talk about Fiat, in a pejorative way.

Fork

A fork (or branch) indicates the development of a new software project that starts from source code in open source environments by a team of programmers. For this type of software licence, no formal permission is required from the original developer. One famous fork is the fork of 1st August 2017, which when people heard that it was about to happen, caused "panic selling" in all the crypto-currencies, throughout the previous month.

Halving

It's the process of reducing the rate with which new crypto units will be generated, that is, they are periodic events that reduce the rewards for block mining. Obviously, more halving leads to the reduction of miners. On BTC they have already occurred in 2012 and 2016, the next will take place in 2020 and will be the third of the thirty-two programmed up to the maximum of circulating bitcoins (21 million pieces). Halving is the basis of the crypto-economic model because it will determine a constant rate of issue, unlike the unlimited national currency without value.

Hash

Any computer document can produce a unique identification of itself, a hash, for which there is no other document producing the same code. The operation to get the identification is called hashing and we will deal with it in the mining section.

Hash rate

Hash derives from the words smudged or messed up and the rate at which this happens is the quantification of the operation. It identifies the computation power of the calculation required by the Bitcoin network to ensure security. When the network reaches a hash rate of 10 Th/s, it means it can make one trillion calculations per second.

ID

It's no other than the complex identification string that identifies the owner of the wallet. In addition to the ID, public keys and an address are required to allow a secure transaction with anyone you want!

Login

It is needed to enter the system, platform or software, and any device that only one person, who holds the correct credentials to keep it safe, uses. In slang, we talk about "logging on" which refers to the insertion of personal codes, to enter safely.

Mining

This is a process in which the hardware of the computer performs mathematical calculations to confirm transactions and it increases the security of the Bitcoin network. The builders of these networks with significant hash rates are the miners and their work is rewarded with new bitcoins that they receive based on the power generated (the more you are useful, the more you are rewarded). They also have the option of directly collecting commission on any transaction that they confirm, but often do not do this. As we will see later, few users are involved in mining and are not an easy way to make money. The main purpose of mining activities is to allow the construction of blocks to confirm transactions and make sure the system is not tampered with.

Node

In computer science, a node is any hardware device in the system that can communicate with other devices that are part of the network. In the crypt, multiple blocks form a Blockchain and they are contained in nodes to aid the calculation speed and the transaction process. Nodes are physical and are made up of huge servers that perform the function of mining.

Open source

It means open source and indicates software whose copyright holders publicize the source code, favouring the exchange of ideas and the possibility to make changes and extensions. It is all regulated by the user licenses. This phenomenon has benefited greatly from the Internet because it allows remote programmers to coordinate and work on the same project. Illustrative examples are Open Office, Android, Linux and Bitcoin. Its design is public, no one owns it or controls it, and everyone can take part in the project. Through some of its unique properties, Bitcoin allows exciting uses that could not be covered by any other traditional payment system.

Peer to peer (P2P)

Translated as a peer-to-peer network, it indicates a logical architecture model network in which there is not a hierarchy of nodes, but they are instead equivalent and equal, which can be used both by a client or a server. Once configured, all nodes are able to initiate or complete a transaction. The classic P2P example is the File Sharing Network.

Private Keys

They are encrypted keys used in an asymmetric encryption system where each private key is associated with a corresponding public key. The characteristic of the cryptosystems is that each pair of keys is formed in such a way that what is encrypted with one can only be deciphered with the other. The two keys are, in the first place, perfectly interchangeable, but the private ones must not be known by anyone other than the owner to legitimize it for the purchase of their bitcoins. When you run a bitcoin transaction, only the public key (address) and not the private one will be visible, which is a long string of more than 30 numbers and letters similar to your bank's IBAN Every time you ask for a new address; you will also change keys, so you will be guaranteed total anonymity!

Proof of work

This is the security protocol to discourage attacks and other abuse of the service, such as spam.

Satoshi Nakamoto

This is the pseudonym of the imaginary and ingenious creator, or set of creators, of the Bitcoin protocol. In November 2008, he published the document "The Cryptography Mailing List" on the website metzdowd.com. In 2009, he distributed the first version of client software and subsequently contributed to the project anonymously with other developers and then retired from the Bitcoin community in 2010. His latest contact occurred in 2011 when he declared that he had gone on to other projects and had Bitcoin's development in the safe and capable hands of Gavin Andresen.

Wallet

An electronic portfolio is a program or more frequently, a web service that allows users to memorize and control their personal information about online purchases centrally and securely. It provides adequate, fast and easy technology that allows the user to purchase products or currencies worldwide. It is also an ever-present container, which contains public keys to make crypto-currency transactions in real time and at very low commissions.

"The true Superstar of the century,
Will be the bitcoin!".

NATIONAL CURRENCY VS BITCOIN

Given the centrality of the differences between national and digital currencies, moreover, to get used to thinking with your own head and with reliable and demonstrable data, I thought of reinforcing the introduction with information in the public domain but that few, very few know.

Well, I introduce the argument with a famous maxim by **Henry Ford**, the great American car magnate, who said that "if *ordinary people really knew how the economic, monetary and banking system works, there would be a great revolution by tomorrow morning*"! I step back a few decades, and in July 1944 in **Bretton Woods**, a town in New Hampshire (USA), the United States decided to win the economic war, even before winning the Second World War. At that time, in a conference open to a few, in addition to the creation of "International Monetary Funds (IMF)", international trade based on the Dollar was regulated and, more importantly, the exchange for physical Gold was set at 35 Dollars/ounce and it was also established that each member country in the face of printed money should have a gold cover held at its national central reference banks. The war ended a year later with well-known winners and losers and the states began to print currency that it was anyway supported, as per agreements, by an adequate quantity of gold reserve.

However, as early as 1960, the French President in office, a certain **Charles De Gaulle**, publicly declared that the circulating Dollars were starting to be a little too much but no one cared because the yellow metal stocks increased hand in hand. With the economic boom, the demand for money became explosive, getting bigger but gold is scarce and they began to feel the first liquidity problems towards the end of the war in Vietnam (1970) where it was necessary to have to print much more to support the bankruptcy war effort. So what did the famous USA President of the moment, **Nixon**, do on 15.08.1971?

Unilaterally, he declared that from that moment the dollar's convertibility into gold was abolished, decreeing the forced extinction of the **gold standard** in favour of the current one, the **floating** one. Do you know what this partisan decision meant and produced? That the value of the currencies would have been determined in a foreign exchange market and more embarrassing, that since then all governments has felt legitimized to be able to print national currency similar to worthless waste paper! Open your wallet and take a banknote, you will notice that it is signed by the President of the Central Bank of reference, it has a "forced course", that is, it is compulsorily accepted even though the value printed on it is not worth the slightest. All citizens are obliged to use national currencies (called Fiat) to buy goods or services, to sell, to do anything.

Now, do you come to tell me that cryptos are not supported by anything? What about Fiat? As already stated, at least the **cryptocurrencies are supported by the trust** of its investors. Be careful because the indiscriminate printing of national currency has led the debt hole to be so large that in the end the central banks and national banks will all fall into it if they do not find a solution soon. Luckily we are going through the known mass phenomenon of **globalization**. It has opened the minds to millions if not billions of people because we finally have a flagless currency that belongs to no nation, no organization, this currency is digital and is called bitcoin! Bitcoin will be the anchor of salvation for the economy world and the sooner you understand it, the better it will be for everyone. He has been legal tender in Japan since 2017 together with the Yen and therefore the door is now open. Bitcoin is unstoppable; it is the new refuge asset in place of Gold. Finally now you should have some truly irrefutable data to better decide whether or not to start investing in crypto.

"Globalization has given us the first flagless currency that does not belong to any nation"!

CHAPTER 1:
WHAT ARE BITCOINS?

In addition to being an innovative protocol, bitcoins belong to the large family of cryptocurrencies (or crypto coins). Unlike traditional coins, they are not physical but only digital, whose implementation is based on the principles of encryption. They allow users to make secure payments online, using P2P sharing technologies. Honestly, the crypt limitations are completely eclipsed by their positive sides, with those features being dealt with in the near future.

Let's start from the assumption that they are coins in all respects because they really perform the typical functions of them. They are like all the others, they can be exchanged, bought, sold, transferred and traded but in addition to this, they can appreciate over time. Have you ever owned a coin that alone is worth thousands of dollars and a year earlier was only worth five hundred? Well, I do! For this reason, I can talk about it calmly, with full knowledge of the facts. Cryptos can pass from one owner to another, without the need for an external body to act as a supervisor between the parties. The banking system here is completely excluded and everyone becomes the manager of their branch located in an unmistakable **"transparent vault"** in which it is possible to see inside but impossible to penetrate and discover the owner. This is a focal and original concept for understanding the phenomenon right now! Any wise investor could accumulate value in cryptocurrency, exchanging Euros for it and keeping it in a secure wallet; at the same time anyone looking at the public register will be able to see all the transactions in that portfolio without any possibility of knowing the name of the owner!

The mechanism is brilliant and you will understand it more and more by continuing reading when eventually the puzzle will be complete. For the time being, you must know that crypt capture is in progress for as long as the cost remains affordable. Everybody wants it, everybody is looking for it, but few know how to do it effectively. There are already many organizations, associations and agencies that accept donations or payments in bitcoin, as well as businesses, universities, post offices, and other institutes that allow crypto compensations. Not only that, but it is even possible to buy them from ATMs, famous portals or from fellow citizens via simple smartphone apps. It will increasingly be a revolution of thought that will turn into changes in everyday life. Becoming aware of this, as soon as possible, could really give you a great competitive advantage towards those who arrive later and certainly late and who, as usual, will regret not having been able to do it before!

THE CHARACTERISTICS TO KNOW

How could you fully understand the capabilities of a car if you do not know all the details about it? The crypts could certainly become a great opportunity to make a profit, but only if you understand the features that make them so special, but at the same time insidious to those who are superficial or presumptuous. Let's see the most important features, which cannot be avoided!

Does the Bitcoin network have a timetable?

Bitcoin is money, and it never sleeps, even during holidays, unlike markets such as Forex! The networks are all compatible with each other, using the same open technology, and the network is always connected globally, without stopping!

Is Bitcoin a consolidated reality?

Absolutely not! It is still an experimental currency in open source development. Its appreciation, use, and demand are concretely high, but to say that it is perfectly safe is certainly not true. Keep in mind that crypts are a relatively recent invention that people are wary of, like everything you know nothing about or that does not give you security (like darkness, death, etc.). For these reasons, I believe that its future is still uncertain, and as such, you have to treat it like that!

Is privacy protected?

The Bitcoin protocol preserves the privacy and anonymity of subscribers, 100%. Subscriptions on any platform for exchanging crypts with national currencies are a little prudent, but guarantee a very high degree of personal security. Even the identity of the parties that complete the transactions is hidden behind a code, still impenetrable at this time. Outside of the crypt world, there is no credit card number that a hacker cannot get to steal your identity. In Blockchain, this becomes much more difficult thanks to the double level of security to enter. Obviously, you have to be careful in protecting your privacy as it is your ultimate responsibility, however, it could be very difficult to discover any fraudulent transactions due to the anonymity in each operation, which makes it difficult to trace the parties involved.

Are Crypto Regulated?

They are not governed by any central bank or authority. They are created in accordance with some computer algorithms and are issued and transferred through a network of Miners and Miners' developers, both of whom are proponents of worldwide popular diffusion and penetration, which so far have been well paid.

Is there a transaction log?

All transactions are collected in a public register and kept permanently. Anyone can see the balance and transactions of any bitcoin address, but cannot detect the identity of the user which is hidden behind a long address of about 30 characters.

Bitcoin addresses should only be used once and then changed, so as not to jeopardize our privacy.

Is the wallet safe?

It will be safe if you keep it safe and you do not adopt unsafe behaviour! The protocol allows the transfer of your assets, everywhere and in a simple way. It allows you control and security thanks to its extraordinary features that require a lot of attention, like the money you have in the bank, nothing more.

Is the bitcoin price stable?

I would not say so! Because of its speculative nature, the new market and the large capital exchanged daily, the price may increase or decrease unpredictably over a short period of time. Do not be fooled into entering all of your savings into crypt, because it is absolutely not recommended. You have to consider crypts as a high-risk investment, so you should deposit 1-5% maximum of your capital, no more! Let's say that as a rule, you should never invest more money than you can afford to lose!

Do transactions last like bank transfers?

Absolutely not! A Bitcoin transaction is instantaneous, but to avoid problems like Double Spending and Scams, you'll have to wait for the transaction to be confirmed, which may take a few minutes. In that period, a transaction can still be reversible and it is at this time that dishonest people act. For example, if you agree to a "live" exchange, after using smartphones to switch currency, you may be fooled by someone saying that they have to go away unexpectedly, but perhaps they have already pocketed the cash before they cancel the transaction. Be vigilant! Before the operation, ask for an agreement in writing or take a photo of the document as a guarantee, so you do not get caught out!

How do you make an exchange?

Exchange operations take place through exchange platforms, which allow the exchange between crypt and fiat, or between crypts, and a record is kept of the transactions made.

Why is the demand high?

The demand is high because they have been designed by placing a ceiling on the amount of coins in circulation, to imitate the shortage of precious metals to increase their value. The rules of the market speak clearly, if the supply is low, the demand increases and obviously so does the price! I will say more, they will probably face what is called deflation, that is, an increase in the perceived real value, pushing it to incredible prices!

Are they favoured by Governments?

They are hunted by governments all over the world! They put the conventional debt system in crisis, giving power to the individual by subtracting it from government control. They tend to decentralize value by not focussing on banks. How could they be favoured? Some governments are creating control bodies to try to stem the phenomenon, but as stated by Bill Gates, Microsoft patron, "Bitcoin will be unstoppable!"

Do cryptos have legislation?

Do not confuse legislation with legality! Unlike national currencies, which are legally named, bitcoin is not supported by any legislation. Paradoxically, if, for example, we witnessed the insolvency of a Central Bank, and conventional systems collapsed, bitcoin could continue to run smoothly as long as there was electricity, to sustain the Internet. However, I want to let you in on some historical news! From 1stApril 2017, the Japanese government was the first to grant recognition to bitcoin, which is now commonly accepted like the Yen. This futuristic choice has already helped improve the Japanese economy, as can be seen from the Nikkei national index chart. Now let me ask you a question I would like you to answer: in your opinion, what will the other states do, because of this?

Are exchange commission high?

Bitcoin is the easiest way to exchange money at a very low cost. In addition, it also allows you to send and receive payments at a very low cost. In fact, excluding special micro payments, there is usually no commission charged, even if it is recommended by the protocol (0.00001 BTC), to remunerate and / or reward miners that guarantee the reliability of the Bitcoin network.

Are crypto durable?

Not all of the current eight hundred and more currencies survive a full economic cycle. The **durability** is higher in those with high capitalization. Therefore, I invite you to only consider the best projects, while I would leave the others to those who do not know what to do with their money!

Are they used by criminals?

The system works discreetly and is growing rapidly both in legitimate and unlawful **recycling** operations, which are difficult to intercept and block. In fact, crypts are currently less susceptible to confiscation by law enforcement thanks to anonymity, thus fostering hundreds of Business and Network Ponzi that I recommend avoiding. With clever behaviour and no risk behaviour, you will never have to worry about anything in any business!

Is the setup to enter the platform easy?

Not particularly, I'll let you know! A platform that must guarantee extreme security and protection to the client must implement all that is in its power to avoid letting the "Coin hacker" in. You will simply have to follow the instructions to the letter, and you will not have any problems.

Can I do operations by smartphone?

You can trade, and pay in two simple steps: Get into the app and receive / send an address or scan a QR code (Quick response code of black and white dots). In the near future we will also be able to use NFC radio technology, by simply connecting two smartphones. Every day we have more news and anticipate that security will increasingly safeguard the use of your personal device.

Are you afraid of digital technology?

You should not be, because you already use plastic cards to pay in a completely digital way, with a click! Personally, I expect that within a decade, all the money circulating will turn into a digital form, like the natural evolution of online transactions. This could stop those who do not pay VAT, as well as taking away the burden of having to print banknotes or mint annoying coins. It is simply the future, and in my opinion, it is the most obvious consequence of today's system!

Is bitcoin the best cryptocurrency?

I have never said that! I stated that it is the most developed and capitalized crypto and dominant (67% at the end of 2019)at least at the moment! For this reason, regardless of the highs and lows in its charts, it continues to expand globally, even though in Europe we are being left behind in exchange volumes. By contrast, countries such as China, Korea, the Philippines and Indonesia are the leaders in the number of transactions and usage. Japan, oddly, was one of the later countries to take this great opportunity on board, but it has already surpassed everyone very intelligently I would say! All the other pseudo-evolved nations, like the EU and US, archaically and stoically, remain as spectators observing the dazzling developments of this phenomenon!

Will shops also accept bitcoins?

It's just a matter of time! As already mentioned, and as I will explain later in the book, more and more companies will accept BTC and Altcoin as an alternative means of payment. Why? Because it would be stupid not to do it! Would you not accept a currency in continuous elevation against the odds? Would you not accept, even partially, a currency that increases its purchasing power against the Euro? Imagine now if I received bitcoins from your sales, a currency that in a few years went from €0.05 to €2,500 and that it doesn't look like stopping there. I'll leave it up to you to come up with your own conclusions!

"Bitcoin will not only be a financial revolution but also one that changes our habits"!

THE GENIUS IDEATOR

One of the few ambiguities pervading the world of crypto-currencies is the system's creator. The fact of not being able to attribute a face to Satoshi Nakamoto creates frustration. Who is this character? How did he create such a thing? Everything is still an enigma today. No one knows whether it is a person, a team or an organization, and what the real purpose of the project was. This mystery can be looked at in two ways: Firstly, the founders do not want to be recognized because they fear repercussions from their own national governments or secondly, behind this phantom Satoshi those institutions that everyone thinks are against the system (but in reality, are thirsty speculators) are concealed. With our current knowledge, the answer is really impossible, but people do not care about this because they are still investing in their digital portfolios in order not to miss out on the chance to get richer with crypto-currencies. I have to admit that the system is really ingenious and I cannot think that it is the result of a single person, the same person who is thought to have a million bitcoins in a maximum of 21 million pieces. Try multiplying a million by the current value of bitcoin and you will realize its financial capacity! Whoever Nakamoto really is, he has caught the attention of millions of people in the world in a few years, rapidly developing an enormous international monetary power. Would you be more interested in knowing how the phenomenon came about or how could you profit from it? Well, the answer would seem obvious!

"With bitcoins, you'll become the bank of yourself, without intermediaries"!
Satoshi Nakamoto

HOW THE PROTOCOL WORKS

By putting together what has been explained so far, we see how a crypto-currency property passage is actually accomplished, leaving aside the creation of new coins and their distribution, because thinking about this at the moment would not help in any way.

We know that every user participating in the Bitcoin network has a personal wallet containing cryptographic pairs of keys. We have identified them as public or private addresses. The former are used as a reference point for sending or receiving sales or purchases. The latter only allows the owner confirmation and unambiguously authorizes the transaction. Addresses are long random sequences, averaging 33 numbers and letters, which always start with the numbers 1 or 3, as in the following example:

185vWty9K4f7NhH5Zx7remF7GQrcHv234T.

As you can see, they are unassigned and completely anonymous. They change continuously and do not contain information about the owner. Every user can always generate new addresses to prevent transactions, which in any case are public, from being traced back to themselves. A new address will be created by simply typing keys like **"send"** if you want to have a currency sent between wallets or private parties, or by typing **"Deposit"** if you want to transfer an amount between your accounts on different platforms using a wire transfer.

Let's take a practical example to facilitate this decisive concept, even if we have already prepared explanatory videos on my YouTube channel that will no doubt help.

I would like to transfer money between two different platforms. Obviously, I can send a certain crypto to receive the same and generally not BTC for Litecoin or anything else. Let's say I wanted to move BTC from A to B. After logging onto both platforms, on platform A, I **"send"** the address previously copied from the **"Deposit"** to Platform B and confirm the move. The transfer is computerised and takes a few minutes for confirmation. In fact, when we run a transaction, it starts in the "unconfirmed" state, i.e. waiting for one or more checks (even 6 for BTC) through a list of hourly markers managed collectively by the famous Blockchain. If the confirmation is successful, we will have the counter value in B and the transactions recorded indelibly. Remember that these operations are irreversible and if something goes wrong in these steps it may result in the loss of the money sent, so these are operations that require your utmost attention. I suggest you first do tests with small values, before going on to a larger sum.

This is what you see on the surface, but if you would like to understand the protocol better, I recommend that you continue reading this paragraph, otherwise go on to the next one.

You should have already learned that each node collects all unsupported transactions in a block chained to a transaction identifier certificate, hash, which is already recognized by the node itself. This requires considerable calculations for the tests to be performed. When the node finds that solution, it announces it to the rest of the network and the peers that receive the block check the validity before accepting it and then adding it to the chain.

When a new transaction is allowed for the first time in a block, it receives a first confirmation. If the block reaches six confirmations, creating six blocks attached to it, the transaction will eventually be confirmed.

Operations that have already been registered **cannot be changed**. It follows that the block chain contains the history of all the movements of all generated bitcoins from their creator's address to the current holder. If we try to reuse an address already sent, the network would inexorably refuse the operation.

*"If your capital can be controlled,
then it is not your capital"!*
Bitcoin Philosophy

THE DIFFERENT TYPES OF CRYPTOS

Virtual coins currently in circulation, like in full gold rush of Klondike, there are over 2400 (given end 2019) and who knows how many will become by the end of the current year. In addition to the king of the crypto-currencies, Bitcoin, the progenitor's protocol, has defined far more than thirty other different which have all been derived from the illustrious parent. It is humanly impossible to look at typologies now, because in a few months it may be an archaic classification and for that reason we will limit ourselves to the data.

Despite the superstar bitcoin being the precursor of crypto-currencies, it is still the market leader. Other cryptos created over the last few years have implemented and improved new technologies. These different cryptos are called **Altcoin** (alternative-coins). Generally, they are marketed as the best substitutes for bitcoin, trying to play down their perceived limitations, always presenting new versions with competitive advantages that attract a share in the market. There is a large variety of Altcoin and intelligently, most, involve mining, extraction processes offering efficient, cheap and just as safe ways to carry out transactions. Of course, even with many overlapping features, Altcoins vary considerably from one another.

The value of Altcoins increased mainly because scrupulous investors wanted to **diversify** using bitcoin to buy more crypto-currencies with alternative designs. In full BTC predominance, I think there are at least three factors to be kept under control to weigh up the real value of crypto-currencies in general, and not just:

- **Perceived Interest**
- **Trading Volumes**
- **Capitalizations**

In the absence of conventional data such as graphic, fundamental and cyclical evidence, this information plays a basic role in understanding what the so-called **"sentiments"** of the market are.

There are already dozens of forums, information sites, private social groups and messaging groups (WhatsApp and Telegram). To help you get started, I recommend two services above all others: the Italian forum **bitcointalk.org** and the site **altcointoday.com.**

The evolution of performance for all crypts is simply as follows. From the data in our possession, we know that the Altcoin "xcoin" has reached an agreement with the world's most famous insurance group to make the payment of the policies through its circuits possible. The dissemination of this news first provokes an escalation of volatility that leads to an **increase in trade** and then turns into an **increase in market capitalization**. Immediate detection of volumes and capitalizations can be searched on many platforms, but I want to point out a site that is specifically designed to solve this problem: **coinmarketcap.com**. Besides ensuring the global capitalization of a single coin this site also distinguishes platforms for it, so you can decide which one to choose when it's time to do so.

Be careful that this site does not process these values in real time but needs at least twenty minutes for processing and viewing. To date, the crypto-currency economy is worth approximately 215 billion dollars globally (end of 2019). If the economy of crypto-currencies has grown so much, its merit is down to the more capitalized currency, the creator of the massive entry of capital into this market. Its importance also lies in the fact that the major exchange platforms (exchanger) basically rely on it for the exchange in Fiat currencies. For this reason, an Altcoin can appreciate in national currencies, only if it gains value over BTC. Sound easy to you? Absolutely not and for this reason 2019 is been a real bloodbath for almost all alternative projects! The scenario is constantly evolving because even now Altcoins are consolidating good exchange volumes. To understand the difference between the BTC and the other cryptos better, let's look at some examples.

-The country with more exchanges between the Fiat national currency and Bitcoin is **Japan**, thanks also to the regulations of 1ˢᵗApril 2017; we talk about trading volumes of Billions of Dollars, while the volume against Altcoins is almost insignificant.

-**China** does not look favourably at BTC, which is used for money laundering, so it prefers Litecoin.

-**South Korea** and its currency (Won) have volumes even higher than the Euro, against Ethereum and then BTC.

-Exchange volumes between Ripple and Fiat are modest, as they mainly trade with BTC.

I believe that anybody could be good at positioning themselves on the market, supported by the high volatility typical of a bubble. However, the "**panic selling**" that began in July 2017 because of the so-called "**Fork**", that is, the War of Protocols, has taught us to decrease the same volatility in the market, inevitably preferring "**fly to quality**", in which only the best projects are rewarded with a fully respected performance in a long-term portfolio.

Ok, but what are the most promising Altcoins to follow carefully? Our choice fell on those who they have tangible projects that are reflected in the excellent exchanges and the major market capitalizations, according to which will be briefly presented, albeit the situation it could change considerably in a few months.

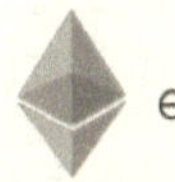

Now, ETH it is the second cryptocurrency in the global panorama after bitcoin. Designed by Vitalik Buterin a Russian mathematical genius, it is nothing more than a public network based on Blockchain. Buterin has achieved a new approach without having to program a new chain of blocks, giving significant technical differences to Bitcoin. Ethereum's success stems from the potential for potentially thousands of different applications in a single platform. Think that Microsoft, Intel, JP Morgan, BP and Samsung have embraced this protocol, and the creator met Putin, announcing some bombshell news and strategic partnership.

ripple

XRP incredibly represents one of the most hated projects by the crypt community, as it is a debit network that has already been used by hundreds of banking institutions to carry out their transactions. Currency is not used to trade value, but as an anti-spam token. The purpose of the Ripple Protocol is in the eyes of many, paradoxical, because, to get rid of commissions, it aims to allow people to get rid of classic payment methods such as credit cards, bank counters, PayPal, etc. but at the same time it is appreciated by the banking system, which has notoriously incorporated these kinds of commissions to survive. Looking forward to future developments, I believe it is a crypt that surely has to be present in a wallet, also thanks to its low cost.

LTC was released shortly after bitcoin, and is famous in the cryptic network because, thanks to its innovative script, it checks transactions in much less time than BTC. It brilliantly reduced the waiting time for the transaction thanks to its innovation, which facilitated the emergence of other cryptos with its "lightness" and speed specifications, even if the bitcoin upgrade could decree its early extinction if it does not enrich its protocol. Well loved by the people in China, who are among its greatest fans, Litecoin is a contender for the best crypt ever.

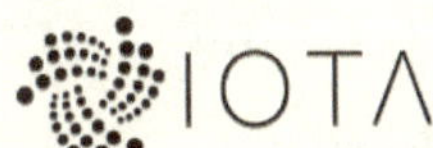

Iota is a brand new and innovative cryptotoken for micro transactions between Internet Of Things (IOT) devices, created to be as light as possible. Devices must be in able to automatically pay tiny amounts, without having to compromise the design of the product. Iota was born for this and, given the amount of exchanges, the creators were right!

 MONERO

We recommend it because, unlike Bitcoin, it was designed to enhance privacy, as it uses an algorithm that eliminates the transcription and traceability process of any transaction in the public registry.

EOS

The EOS Blockchain aims to become a decentralized operating system that supports industrial-scale applications with the intent to completely remove transaction fees and the ability to manage millions of operations per second. It is a sure success coin and is permanently in the high end!

Stellar Lumen

XLM is an open source currency exchange protocol found in 2014, supported by a large funding foundation. Several non-profit organizations are implementing it as a financial structure. He announced many partnerships, especially in emerging countries. Finally, it was chosen by IBM as the technology to be used for international payments!

As you have seen, there is one crypto-currency for each type of use, although most investors think they are all the same. Before considering the purchase should check its characteristics, the capitalization in the top 20, the management, the site with **the roadmap**, that is, the temporal sequence of actions envisaged in achievement of one's goals and sentiment market, to turn your choices into real business high performance.

"Altcoins an alternative investment".

CHAPTER 2:
HOW TO MAKE A PROFIT?

Finally, we enter the second part of the book, that training, the one in which I will propose models for you definitely move to personal action! I think you understand that those who are holding effective knowledge, they might think in a way optimistic about their future. Mindful of this universal teaching, advice to avoid haste e take some time to exercise the power of the three fundamental pillars! Cryptos and bitcoin in particular, are generally in the phase of planetary and non-planetary appreciation I speak only of value. Between ups and downs, capitalizations they would tend to rise, although in the future it is not said that keep doing it! In general, the greatest potential for gain is represented by their **possession**. Creating a personal portfolio in crypto-currency is absolutely the best idea to "accumulate value", such as buying gold bullion was in the recent past. Let's see which systems can be adopted to make money as soon as possible and as much as possible. A **"step by step"** step should take the following steps into account.

1- **Properly know** in special channels e competent, on how crypto protocols work, such as are the characteristics to know, such as the types and the sorting of the best, as we mentioned in the first chapter of this work.

2- **Be informed about** the chances of gain you could get, by reading the continuation of the reading.

3- **Choose the most suitable platforms** for you, according to what you have defined and planned to build. Do not forget that these will be the tools to buy a cryptos and seeing the tremendous and abundant offers on the web I will help you choose, according to your needs and your goals.

4- **Get crypto-currency**, by going through the following actions, using the various methods I will explain, including:

-**Exchange**, i.e. **currency exchange**, is certainly the simplest, most direct and widespread method for acquiring crypto, through conversation markets and dedicated platforms that allow you to exchange bitcoins or other crypto currencies using traditional currency through various payment types.

-**Lending,** if you are short of capital, you can use the loan, for the payment of a monthly fee, which we will see in more detail in the third chapter.

-**Mining**, which is nothing other than the process of building a Blockchain node for which you could receive considerable rewards, but only with good computer skills, enough capital, considerable space, and a great deal of electrical contract.

-**Register for free** at sites that offer small fractions of the crypto (negligible), performing tasks such as clicks, games, ratings, network construction, etc.

5- **Saving Crypt** to create a prodigious **value reserve**, and if you own an entrepreneurial business, you may also consider accepting, bitcoin partially or wholly, for the payment of your goods or services. There are already many forward-looking professionals who have cleverly approved this system to accumulate bitcoin in their wallets. Do not waste time and ask your tax advisor for this possibility.

6- Learn to **invest part** of what you have set aside, to multiply your earnings, through systems like:

-**Mining** on behalf of third parties, where you do nothing but rent a portion of the computing capacity to others, for which you will receive a monthly or daily payment in crypt.

-**Trading**, i.e. currency trading, taking advantage of the ups and downs on the graphs or the volatility of the market. Be careful, however, this is not for everyone, for you may risk losing all your money.

-**Participation in I.C.O.** (Initial Coin Offering) surfing the huge wave of full euphoria that deals with the offerings of new and future coins on the market.

7- **Manage your wallet** with eagerness, as I think you already do with your portfolio and money deposited in your traditional bank.

8- **Hold** and then maybe spend part of the purchasing power later since it was developed to be a quick, easy and cost-effective means of spending, and not just for speculation.

Finally, let's go into each of these possibilities to find the one that best suits your needs!

"The value of each bitcoin is unstoppable,
it could even reach $ 100,000". Bill Gates

SET ASIDE VALUE ON THE WALLET

To start setting up a reserve value, we need to know how to get hold of cryptocurrency. We have already explained that the easiest and most direct way to get it is through a common online exchange known as a **"Wallet"** which is nothing other than a site impenetrable by a third party, which allows a simple **"currency change"**, that is, a safe exchange between Euros deposited in our bank, and a pre-selected cryptos. A wallet in this case electronic is used to place your crypto value reserve in, allowing you to deposit, store, receive and send currency to other wallets or other exchanges. It will be like your bank deposit account, like an armoured box that only you can open, which will become our own bank. You have understood well! It will be your own bank because there will not be any branches or brokers. You will have your own currency without trading opportunities, but you can order other types of inbound or outbound operations to other platforms. Such secure environments and secure transfers will only be allowed by using addresses like IBAN/BIC, totally inaccessible to fearsome "Coin hackers" thanks to the advanced Blockchain technology.

With a wallet on a suitable **"Exchange"** platform, you will have a personal treasure chest and you will have to use it regularly to convert programmed amounts of Fiat currencies into a crypto, by firstly setting aside a preference for its majesty the bitcoin. Such exchange can take place after the **following steps** (recover sheet and pencil):

-You have chosen the most suitable type of payment for you, between bank transfer, credit card (preferably rechargeable), payment processors, PayPal, or paying personally with an app, etc.

-You have chosen the first platform most relevant to your type of payment, for currency exchange;

-You have created your new wallet, going through registration and all security levels, including a two-factor authentication, to safeguard the deposit;

-You have determined the amount of money to be transferred and have already uploaded it to the selected media;

-You have waited for the best price conditions, maybe later a sudden drop in the prices of the currency from to exchange.

-You have written a medium to long term collection strategy in the style of an Accumulation Plan, similarly to those when depositing in traditional banks, such as Common Funds and E.T.F.

Only after these necessary evaluations and careful planning will you be able to think of having your first wallet without making mistakes and without any surprises. Each action follows an appropriate assessment, not just here, but in all areas of life. Think about it!

"Set aside value for years,
and you will have treasure"!

HOW TO CHOOSE A WALLET

The offer is really huge and I would not want to confuse you! There are Web and Desktop versions for each operating system, versions for each smartphone, as well as offline versions like physical hardware, and so on!

This data is constantly evolving, as the range of available services on a daily basis is being expanded. In general, you should be careful that the wallet uses **"decentralized confirmation"** because if it was centralized, you could be entrusting third parties who might hide or simulate payments that have not occurred. For this reason, the main wallets I recommend are the ones I have already tested. They are: **Blockchain.info**, Bitstamp.net, Bitcoin Wallet, Bread wallet, Green Bits, Green Address, Electrum (Desktop) and Ledger Nano S (Hardware external). How to help you choose? I advise you to consult the updated information on the Official Site of Bitcoin.org Italia.

Generally speaking, if you start from zero and work with values up to€10,000, start with Blockchain.info to practice with, because it is a **web version** with simple graphics, crucially only concerning bitcoin exchanges and it is extremely safe. Remember that each movement of money **will have a commission fee** to pay based on the total amount of the payment. It is usually a small percentage, specified in the conditions of each exchange.

Later on, with more experience, you may feel the need to remodel your choices, even though it is not obligatory. I'm giving you more information than is necessary at this point, so that you will not be unprepared in the future. During the initial registration process, you will immediately notice that it may seem pretty intrusive, even though it is modulated to ensure maximum security. There are wallets that have eliminated long and laborious identity verification procedures, where you do not even have to sign up for an account thus completely avoiding tracking and identification.

Among these, we have portals like **Indacoin** or **Bitit**, which are among the fastest when buying, but also among the most limited in terms of the amounts, you can trade. You just need to sign up to get started in buying up to € 100 in bitcoin or Ethereum with a Visa or MasterCard credit card, getting discounts on subsequent purchases. Personally, I do not recommend them because I prefer absolute security, to not find myself with nothing to show for my effort, maybe after months of accumulation! In addition, I was convinced that wallets could only be found online, but I was wrong! If you have capital of over € **10,000** in crypt, I recommend you evaluate **Electrum**, which is a downloadable version on PC or Mac, so it can be used offline. For considerable capital, Hardware versions in the form of **usb keys** with LED display are also emerging, which are also possible to use offline, for maximum anti-intrusion. **The Ledger Wallet Nano** is one of these miniaturized technological finds, in which you can store bitcoin or any other digital, encrypted and secure coin that you can always carry with you. Think about how it allows you to manage your wallet by connecting to a PC, or with a tap directly from its mini display. It is protected by a pin code, and it is possible to do a full backup to avoid losing crypt in case of hardware breakage or loss. It has a cost that is truly accessible to everyone and it did not occur to you to buy it used, because the old owner holds the keys he could use in his favor, emptying your wallet in a millisecond!

Finally, for the record, on your way you will run into wallets that allow the construction of networks and that thanks to each user brought to the site registration, you will be able to receive 50% "Revenue Share" commissions for payments from your affiliates. Be very careful because you are advising your friends about a possible investment already dangerous self, but if on a network, it becomes even more so

.

"The platform is like a tailored dress,
tailor-made, for each person"!

HOW TO JOIN WITHOUT FEAR

Have you chosen the wallet platform closest to your needs? Yes? Well, you can go ahead and open a new electronic wallet to start setting up a value reserve with a crypt.

On **YouTube** channel, there are already videos that can help you with these first and important steps.

For a new wallet in Blockchain, photo IDs and a recent utilities bill will obviously not be necessary. However, they will be needed for the second great step in opening a second platform suitable for Exchange, but in this case, between bitcoins and other cryptos.

Each wallet has its own fairly complicated access system, but don't worry, they are pretty easy to understand and work out. If they are not in your first language, you can right-click on the page, translating everything, using a browser like Google Chrome.

At the end of the initial registration, wallets strongly advise you to raise the level of security with the use of "two-factor authentication (**2fa**)".

This significantly increases security from the risk of intrusion because it requires a password and a second form of identification that is often issued by a smartphone app such as Google **Authenticator**. To activate this function simply download it onto your phone, open it and scan the **"QRCode"** square, which will result in a six-digit code, which constantly changes. You will need to insert this code into the wallet quickly because a timer will show you how many seconds you have available before the new code appears.

I strongly advise you to save your long alphanumeric codes (secret keys) near the QR Code in external PC or back up files, because if you change your smartphone, you should first reset the keys otherwise you may be unable to access your wallet (if you do not have a "clone phone" service), you may need to open a support ticket and that may take several days to resolve the issue.

Recapping useful but not obligatory steps:

-Complete the initial signup for opening a new wallet;

-Activate a two-factor authentication to increase your account security;

-Add a PIN for withdrawals, if required;

-You are ready to proceed if there are ideal exchange conditions;

-Welcome to the select club of digital currency holders.

*"Fear is generated by
the lack of awareness of your means"!*

THE FIRST TRANSACTION

The exchange of cryptos must include a pull back, a downgrade, call it what you want, but the price will have to be tempting, otherwise you should think twice about it. A bitcoin exchange is really simple. If you've explored the wallet, even on a mobile app, you'll notice that you have just two possibilities: **send or receive**. You cannot go wrong with such simplicity. If you are on your first transaction, there will be maximum limitations due to money laundering. Click on receive, and prepare for the Euro payment to be exchanged for BTC, through the appropriate interface that gives you several possibilities. The question: What payment method will I use? You can certainly use a bank or post office account card, especially a **rechargeable** one. There is a way to buy bitcoin through **PayPal**, but this is currently subject to very high commissions, and is not worth it.

We'll go on to see that you can already buy bitcoin from private owners, even through PayPal but without commission. Be careful, however, that there are a lot of scams around, but more so for sellers.

An **example of a scam**: You the buyer pay to receive bitcoins, you get them but then file a claim to PayPal saying that you have not received anything, and the seller doesn't say anything because the transaction has not been validated! Purchase will only be possible if the seller is sure the buyer does not file a claim to PayPal to receive a refund of the payment made. Who gives you the guarantee? No one, so start by using conventional and reliable systems!

Use a rechargeable bank card, if you don't want to make an international wire transfer that will make you wait more days to be completed.

Always remember that bitcoins do not really exist, they are electronic traces of transactions and people are always trying to trick you.

Now that we have completed the first pay out in the wallet, let's see how to transfer bitcoins, or a portion of them:

-Between two platforms of the same person, for example, a wallet and another exchange platform for Altcoins.

-Between two different people, with different platforms.

How are they sent?

It's harder to explain than to actually do it! If we first used the "receive" button for the first payment, we will now use the **"Send"** button. We will call "X" and "Y" the two parties in the transaction. **If X would like to pay Y** you should proceed in this way:

-Receiving subject Y clicks "Receive" on the wallet and produces the so-called "input address", consisting of the long code that we have previously dealt with, to get the determined amount of bitcoin.

-Subject X receives the address from Y even if it is called "output" to send the amount agreed for the transaction.

-Subject X proceeds by entering the code and sending it by clicking on the correct button. All you have to do then is to wait for confirmation that the transaction has been processed. Meanwhile, you cannot start any new operations.

To be more practical, for example if you want to make a transfer from your wallet to the Exchange, enter the address generated by the Exchange into your wallet and run the order. Conversely, if you want to transfer a sum to your wallet from your exchange, enter the generated address from the wallet into your exchange and run the order.

Simple isn't it? You could also try it out with the Blockchain app on your phone to practice!
Finally, do not wait for any **receipt**, it is not foreseen, but in the wallet, you will be able to verify each transaction in chronological order with all the commission, if they have been requested.

"If you made the first transaction,
you did the hardest thing, congratulations"!

EXCHANGING CRYPTO

As you will understand in the next paragraph devoted to practical strategies, to quantify crypto value, bitcoin is not enough. To have maximum potential, I would say, you will have to include a second platform with your wallet: a new **exchanger** of many other currencies, to let you into the colourful cryptic world.

Basically, even the wallet itself is an exchanger, because it also serves to exchange a Fiat (national) currency with a crypt to hold (**Hold** or Hodl) in portfolios, but here we will talk about other types of currency exchange that will allow you to implement more mobile and in some ways even more powerful systems with Altcoins. Are you ready for the second big step? Well, you should already be able to register on a platform. In these other platforms that we call "**Exchange to Move (ETM)**", because of international anti-money laundering laws, you will find a new phase of identification for which you will have to prepare for and keep available:

-Photo ID (photo with a white background);

-A recent household billin colour, which is no older than ninety days;

-A recent personal photo, if possible.

After several attempts and after dozens of tickets open at the desks of the managers, I can safely say that the best EtM platforms, the most secure, versatile, fast and multifaceted although not yet perfect, they are: Bittrex and Binance. To the moment, a special mention, but second, the deserve platforms like the rock trading, Kraken, Bit shares, while Poloniex I use it only to view the charts quickly.

Let's summarize the operations to be performed:

-Sign up for a new account on chosen platform;

-Enter the required documents, because each one has its own requirements;

-In case of problems, do not delay in asking for assistance that is what they are paid for;

-Activate the two-factor authentication to increase your account security and the pin for withdrawals;

-Proceed as explained above, testing transfers with small amounts, from the wallet to the EMT, with the button "receive" or **"Deposit"**;

-Be careful not to confuse currencies; if you send BTC, you need to receive BTC and nothing else, because if you make a mistake, you could lose the transaction and money;

-Before exchanging Altcoin, watch some videos about it.

All transfer procedures go from a wallet or to a wallet. Practice moving crypt and you'll be ready to apply the opportunities in the next paragraph.

The choice of platforms will be entirely personal, but I wanted to tell you about the ones mentioned above because:

"I don't want you to make
the same mistakes I made!".

PRACTICAL STRATEGIES

These upcoming systems derive from my twenty-year experience in trading. I don't want to talk about very difficult methods, simply because I do not know your technical background, and I do not want to bore you with things that are too difficult to understand.

Strategies will be closely linked to diversification, depending on the platforms that are being used. First of all, we start with the **"Exchange to Hold"** wallets, the platforms in which we signed up to exchange Fiat currency into crypt, to keep in portfolios. Holding, i.e. keeping bitcoin firmly in the wallet, in these times of a worldwide boom in bitcoin, could certainly represent a great system to increase the value of our personal reserve. For example, if we exchange and buy a bitcoin for a value of € 1000, we wait a few months and then sell it back at € 2000; we will get a 100% net gain between buying and selling. Nothing different from buying any other financial instrument! This with all due respect, can only happen by having the capital and getting the **timing** right for the exchange.

Bitcoin, according to major financial analysts in the world, is not going to grant you 100%, but much more in the years to come. You just have to avoid being impatient and rushing in to make a profit like most Italians do. In business, 20% is technical, but 80% is psychology, so I think the strategy of **holding** is really rewarding especially when it comes to the lowest entry prices on the market.

If you do not can read the price chart, or do not have time to spend on Timing, I would advise you to practice a "**CAP**" style strategy, that is, as if you had started a long-term **Capital Accumulation Plan** where every month, you'll put a portion of your savings into the wallet, which you do not need. By doing so, you would avoid various controls and your work would essentially be set aside. This is the most used system by most global investors, who define themselves as prudent.

If I wanted to raise the board, I would recommend you think in BTC because the platforms are **"bitcoincentric"**, it is set as a reference for everything, not the dollar, the euro, etc. By reasoning in BTC right away, you will scroll down some computational steps that might confuse you, and it will be much better and faster having the bitcoin as a point of reference.

The next advice is to sign up for some **ETM** platforms, to move the value reserve. Please follow this practical example carefully.

Imagine you've stored a bitcoin in your wallet. You also register on Bittrex and decide to transfer over 50% of the crypto: 0.5 BTC. Click on deposit in Bittrex, you generate the public address you will enter in the "send" wallet, authorize it and you will find yourself with half a bitcoin to "move" on the ETM. This is a great system, which we call **"diversification"**. It consists of selecting the best Altcoins, for example five, and dividing into them the available amount of BTC on the second platform. In the example, math s shows that you have to divide 0,1 bitcoins for each currency, then proceed with the exchange of each of them. With 0.1 BTC you can buy: 2.000 Ripple, 100.000 Dogecoin, 1 Ethereum, 100 Litecoin and 100 Stratis. With such an operation you will have greatly multiplied your chances of success, by diversifying in more quality currencies. Monthly payment may also be mediated or split between the two platforms, but I will let you in on another secret. As you have already understood, the real trick is to **pay very little for them and get a lot back in return,** because every slight variation on the rise in value will result in a positive performance. If you buy 100,000 pieces of Dogecoin at 0.000001 BTC and hypothetically after six months, the price rises to 0.01 do you know how much you will have earned? Do the calculations and you will be astonished!

Let's assume that after a few months, the price of the five Altcoins literally exploded! What do you have to do? A good investor always has making a profit as a first goal: the return of the investment that is called **"Break Even (BE)"**! The rules say to get your investment money back and let your profits run without risk! If you were not interested in getting back your initial investment, in order to not reduce your multiplying profits, it would also be understandable because it was defined a priori as "expendable"!

You could convert a portion of your profits into BTC and keep it in the wallet; you could further **diversify** into other Altcoins; you could buy new currencies (ICO); could think about starting a buy-sale of Altcoin on sentiment to be settled after a few days with gain (topic of our next book: Trading),or you could use the **"Pump"** Strategy when you are more familiar with Bittrex. This strategy exploits the euphoric effect of mass buying by a cohesive group of people who receive a unique input signal for a given Altcoin. There are so many **Telegram** groups, some with even several thousand members, who take advantage of this method. Let's take an example. Imagine being one of twenty thousand people to receive a message at 6pm to enter "Xcoin"; fooled by ignorance you enter the market with a predetermined quantity, getting in there before many others who will follow the "pumping" effect. The Result: Those who issued the signal were already in the market, so they earn much more than others do, but even those who arrived later have very respectful performances even increasing by several percentage points. If this process was implemented every day, you could achieve high monthly returns without having to do any analysis even if speed is a key element of the method. Not everyone there they will earn, or rather many will lose us and for this reason I recommend paying close attention to such methods, to be tested only when a certain confidence with the orders on the platform has been taken.

These are just small examples of strategy and foolproof methods, but it will always depend on your operating plan, from what you are looking for, from your risk appetite, from the time you have available and the hunger you have. It will be mine care to provide you with a shared document on Google Drive, to facilitate both your project planning and private updating of our strategies. Imagine now, what could happen if you hold these long-term currencies in portfolios? All got with modest investment and without thanking anyone else if not yourself!

"Diversify and you will multiply your earnings"!

TAXATION

Most of the questions that I get asked in private are: "Is the purchase legal? How are the cryptocurrencies taxed? " Let me explain it to you immediately with a practical example!

You have to go to England for work. You change €120 and get £100. Meanwhile, the sterling appreciates a lot and on your return, you will change the same £100 back into Euros receiving €150. Is this capital gain taxed? No, why? Because it's a simple currency exchange! The same for crypto! OK, but bitcoin is not an official currency! Don't worry! It is ok that most legal systems require income tax, sales tax, capital gains tax, and taxes on wages, but it is not the case for bitcoin. Who sets it up? In the euro zone, the European Banking Authority (European ABI for Equity in Italy) declared the free exchange of digital currencies without any limitation or taxation in 2014 because it is comparable to a normal currency exchange. Therefore, the investment in bitcoin, despite fluctuations, at least from a purely fiscal point of view, could be really very convenient! If something should change in the future, I will certainly deal with it on my channels! The only black cloud on the horizon is represented by the **IRS** (Internal Revenue Service), the USA government's tax collection agency which supervises this phenomenon and has ample powers to investigate tax evasion, since it can ask counterparties to disclose personal information, including passwords, for investigative purposes. What would happen if it also came to Europe? Only those who use cryptos to hide something would be afraid. Remember that those who have a clear conscience never need to be afraid!

Finally, I just wanted to remind you of your exclusive responsibility in buying and selling crypto. However, I recommend that you contact your tax advisor to confirm or refute what I have said in relation to the relevant laws I have mentioned above.

"Bitcoin is now recognized all over the world"!

CHAPTER 3:
WHAT IS LENDING?

Lending platforms are sites where you can **borrow from someone or lend** bitcoin **to someone**. They are ideal portals if you do not have investment potential with eligible capital, or if you want to diversify your investment, lending already owned crypto, to third parties. It is a phenomenon that is growing rapidly and we should not fail to investigate it further.

As in the banking sector, the borrower agrees to a specific interest rate from the creditor to obtain the BTCs. Those who decide to finance the fund receive a constant monthly income of a few percentage points, so that everyone is happy.

Let's change perspective! In return, these sites accept bitcoins from lenders, which are then invested, lending them to borrowers who pay monthly installment plus interest, as in any other loan. It is a form of investment for lenders, a form of cheap procurement for borrowers and intermediate companies eat up the commission!

Lending is offered by global companies operating in peer-to-peer mode. Registration only takes a few minutes and you may access your first bitcoin investment in a short time if you have the required guarantees. They are completely free sites and you will not have to pay any commission or a monthly payment, because a profit is made between the difference of the loan and the return, such as traditional loan agencies.

Why apply for a Bitcoin loan? If you have a new business idea or you want to start at ETM or Trading, or you want to build a Bitcoin node for autonomous mining, or you want to consolidate your business, etc. The **platforms** structure the whole process as fairly and as transparently as possible. Here are some **advantages** over normal financial ones:

-There is no subscription cost, either as a borrower or as a lender;

-They have interest rates that are better than traditional providers, generally between 1 and 6%;

The granting of credit is much faster;

-The investor gets a better R. O. I. (return on investments), up to 5.5% per month, in a stable and non-fluctuating manner like those with hold-in wallet annuities;

-Approval is manual and non-electronic; to reduce the possibility of fraud and it takes a few days with all the minimum guarantees, even if this does not completely eliminate the risk!

The best Lending companies are **Bitbond**, **BtcPop**, **XCoins**, **BitLendingClub**, and **Poloniex**. For up-to-date information about the reliability of these sites, please consult: **coinstaker.com.**

What do you have to do to get a loan?

You need to be in one of the supported countries and make your profile more reliable, so that more lenders can trust you to lend you bitcoins. Here is a list of criteria, which will be subject to review, to improve your perceived reputation:

-Check the recognition document, credit card and phone number;

-You have to look like a real person and not a ghost on your social profiles like Twitter, Facebook, LinkedIn, etc;

-Get connects to PayPal, Amazon, EBay, etc.

-Be realistic about what your real income could be!

In short, nobody would like to be cheated! That is obvious. If the lender does not receive the monthly repayment of the loan, the Company will initiate an international arbitration procedure, which will sue the borrower for the promised money.

I have already accumulated several bitcoins what do I have to do if I wanted to become a financier? Here are some tips:

-Include lending in your work of diversifying crypto capital (10-20%);

-Do not accept people with a bad reputation, those who do not have feedback or those that are asking for loans for the first time;

-Check out the person and the reasons for their request, before granting the loan;
-Better to invest in many applicants with small quantities than with only one applicant, even if they are high-profile;
-The interest rates offered by the borrower are an indicator of risk, the higher the rate, the greater the risk;
-Don't choose the "AutoInvest" function, it would be suicide;
-Don't invest more than you would be able to lose!

Carefully weigh up both lending possibilities; it could be a good opportunity. Imagine that you have to pay 5% per month for the loan, and that you make 50%! On the contrary, imagine if you could receive 5-10% or even more annuities a month for life, regardless of the trend in cryptos!

*"If you can't buy, evaluate lending,
If you don't want to risk, lend".*

CHAPTER 4:
HOW TO MINE NEW COINS?

Mining (from the verb "to mine" i.e. to extract) means simply appropriating generated and randomly released portions of Bitcoin from the network. To receive them, it would be necessary to equip oneself with high cost technological instrumentation, capable of generating considerable computing power. The higher the power, the higher the chances you will get from the network! You will need large funds to procure suitable warehouses and large PCs, huge servers, Guiminer software, mining equipment (also sold on EBay), kits to raise computing power and configuration and the ability to cover huge costs for electricity and local specialized personnel. For this reason, miners of a certain level are often located in countries that favour this business such as Iceland, Bulgaria, the UK and Eastern countries, etc.

While conventional money systems print new currency with no intrinsic value and issue it through the central banks, the ingenious Nakamoto has devised a reward system to solve the problem of how to gradually introduce, new digital currency into circulation: by using a Blockchain, the chain of blocks. The system is designed to "donate" bitcoin to the miners, as a prize because they provide processing power to fortify the chain, distributing new bitcoins in proportion to the added power. In simple terms, the work of the miner is to take all unconfirmed and recorded transactions, transcribe them on a block and specify the address where his prize should be sent as a consideration for the work done. The prize is earned, if the miner finds the **hash** of this block, plus a series of zeros (nonce), through which the randomly placed nodes of the net consider the degree of difficulty of the extraction. If the mining's computational power is remarkable, the higher the probability is of finding the hash with the "nonse", before others. Once the hash with the node has been found, the Blockchain

chain is confirmed and the miner is finally rewarded!

Those who have been doing this for years can now boast thousands of bitcoins in their wallets and you only have to look at today's headlines to see the riches we are talking about! Now the system is self-regulating and has drastically reduced the average daily gain per machine, because costs are rising. This has cleverly encouraged miners to join the so-called **"mining pools"**, to guarantee a more constant flow of money than just mining individually. To make you understand the order of earnings, know that in 2019 the most important pool (BTC.com) earned well 26 million dollars. To be concise, we have essentially identified **two types of Mining**:

- With Hardware
- Without Hardware

Mining with hardware is the one carried out by purchasing all the above-mentioned instrumentation, to personally compete in getting the premiums, but as specified, it's about investments of a certain scale with really high costs, that would be unthinkable in Italy, but possible just outside the borders!

Mining without hardware, i.e. without a calculator, could be done in two ways:

- With an installable software
- Online

The former is simple software downloadable onto Windows on your PC, Mac, tablet or iPad, or from certain websites, and it allows you to contribute to computing power. There are thousands of them, but it is better to look into them before downloading them. Your computer should work uninterruptedly for the duration: but is it worth the cost? Most of the time, NO! Try to download **Miner gate** by way of an example and you will realize that you can earn a small commission of 1.5% on the coins that you will help to create, severely limiting the potential of your PC, for other things. Even with the "Smart Miner" function, the program will automatically undermine the most profitable crypto-guidelines of the moment, but try it out and let me know if it was worth it!

Mining Online was came about from a completely different premise: rent a portion of computing power from companies that already do mining, who then reinvest your money. This phenomenon is called **"Cloud mining"** and by investing as much as you like even a few tens of Euros to start with, you can buy a package to "rent" capacity of your choice. The larger the investment, the greater the calculation and capital creation capacity which often takes about six to eight months to **break-even** on the investment. There are annual, biennial or long-term packages. You'll mine both bitcoin and Altcoins. Many consider them to be scamming Networks, but the low initial investment of your choice and regular payments, even daily, can certainly appeal to many people and become a good method of diversification at low cost.

Finally, to benefit from the power of mining without having available funds, I'll tell you about another myriad of sites that favour **free online mining**, allowing you to carry out various activities such as games, polls and viewing advertising videos, etc. Of course, everyone allows paid upgrades to increase extraction capacities, but at this point, I would prefer the previous ones.

Among the myriad of sites that offer this kind of mining, I have personally embraced some of them, but I would not want to mislead you and I advise you to consult coinstaker.com on the Cloud mining page for better and more up-to-date information than mine.

Do you understand now why there are dozens of sites in which you can subscribe to mining, even for free? To increase its computing power, perhaps reinvesting the payments of subscribers, to aspire to succulent rewards in bitcoin, giving the crumbs to us lenders!

"If you think of mining as a way to diversify even more, you are well informed"!

CHAPTER 5:
HOW TO TRADE?

The term "trading" derives from the verb "to trade", which means marketing, buying and selling. The main differences with the operations we have seen so far, lie in the fact that as well as being able to buy just before prices go up   it is also possible to use the **leverage technique**, which is notoriously useful for multiplying the capacity for profit gain, but at the same time there is also a risk of making a loss. Trading is not a game! Do not approach it lightly because you might experience a significant loss in a few nanoseconds.

As a trader I'll tell you that the current platforms, which we will call **EtT (Exchange to Trade)**, are not really within everyone's reach, also because of the different ways in which they operate. Moreover, perhaps for their young age, I assert that only a few are efficient (like BitMex that has also of Demo but it is without "underlying"), so I think that the ideal conditions for mass use are intended for only a few. This is my personal opinion, but exploring them might still be a good idea.

For informational purposes only, to start thinking about trading, you'll have to transfer portions of your account into Bitcoin or other cryptos from other platforms, as we've already seen in the previous examples. Nothing else!

Be careful though; don't confuse these EtT platforms with the **Brokers**. These are experts in other speculative instruments such as Forex and other options, but they are not (yet) exchangers because they allow trading in **C. F. D. (Contract for Difference)**, and not "pure" cryptos. So, open your eyes and don't lose sight of your objectives, swamping yourself with brokerage commissions and spreads. Remember CFDs are one thing and crypt is another. The famous Broker platforms are: Plus500, Market.com, Avatrade, etc.

I think that our priority of trading in cryptos should be focused first of all on learning how to buy them and not selling them. If you really have to sell it, liquidate only a portion of it, if it is positive.

If you are a neophyte, a "newcomer" in terms of crypto, the only type of trading that you will be granted is the "Buy low and Sell high" one, i.e. buying when the price is low and reselling when it is high! This alone is the most effective way to increase your savings, with moderate risk! Crypto trading is very speculative, so let's leave that to the true professionals in the sector, or think about it after you have reached a good degree of awareness and practice, perhaps through our next book on this topic!

The real big difference between those who want to accumulate to "protect their backs" and those who want financial freedom, is one thing: **speed!** Without trading, it will probably take some time to set aside a certain amount of money, but start trading and you will only have a 5% chance of seeing the light at the end of the tunnel. Make your choices with courage and wisdom!

Finally, according to the US news, we know that despite the resistance of the SEC, there could soon be the first ETFs in the crypto field, an excellent additional risk diversification tool!

*"Trading is for a few people,
but those few are finally free!".*

TYPES OF ORDER

For all those who are familiar with trading platforms, I will simply give you a brief overview of the types of orders that can be placed on the platform. Orders are divided into two groups:

- **Unconditioned;**
- **Conditioned.**

The unconditioned Order, which, as the word itself says, has no conditions; it is the most used and simplest order because it enters the market at the moment we click the "send" button. There are many names, but perhaps you know it as "at best" or "at the market".

The best time to use an order of this kind, is when you want to enter or exit an instrument quickly, especially using the "book" which in the crypt market is also visual and takes the name of "market depth", depicted as two, red and green icebergs of orders that collide, to generate the market price.

The conformation of the two will make you understand if green orders, in purchase (also called **Bid**, price on Offer) are predominant, or vice versa, if the red orders, for sale (also called Ask, price required) are predominant.

These types of orders could be classified as **Long** (purchase) or **Short** (sale), after choosing the **"size"**, the entity at the margin of the operation and the **"leverage"**, i.e. the multiplication coefficient.

The Conditioned Order can be of different types and with many different denominations. These are purchase, or sale orders set by the trader on the platform and automatically sent to the market when a specific condition occurs. Until this condition is met, the order remains on the server. The most common way of using Conditioned Orders is to **stop loss** (to limit losses) and/or **take profits** (to cash in on earnings). The automation allows you to free yourself from the constant monitoring of the market when you are not at the computer. For these reasons, they could serve both the active

Trader, allowing him to be more efficient and automated in the control of numerous open market positions, and the occasional investor allowing him to free himself from the need for constant monitoring of the market. Other conditional orders are the **"Limit"** and the **"Stop"** ones, which we will not go into here. Finally, remember that every transaction generates a commission and that is why we should try to use them as little as possible. For real trading, there are inbound commissions of about 0.15%, while outbound ones are up to 0.25%.

BE CAREFUL OF VOLATILITY

Volatility is improperly associated with the term **"speculative bubble"**. In fact, volatility is the measure of the percentage change in the price of a financial instrument over time. (Wikipedia) The speculative bubble is a particular phase of the market characterized by a considerable and unjustified increase in prices, due to a sharp and rapid growth in demand. Subject to this appropriate distinction, volatility measures the evolution of the bubble phenomenon. You can't hope to perform well, while being away from the bubbles. It is impossible! They are not extraordinary exceptions, but they are entirely normal economic phenomena that serve to support trade. They are the natural proof of innovation in most diverse sectors, such as the web boom since 1990, Tech since 2000 and crypto since 2010. If you didn't take advantage of the enormous added value of a bubble, you would lose the chance of accumulating enough money to dignifiedly face the next bubble (perhaps robotics).

The "**crypto bubble**" shows impressive volatility. Just look at the BTC chart from its inception to see that the price fluctuates like a rollercoaster. In, In January 2017 it reached $1,000, in May $2,000, in June almost $3,000 and in July, it fell to $1,931, on December 17, 2017 it reached its all-time high at $ 20,000 and then relentlessly collapsed until 3120 in October 2018.Given its nature, tomorrow we do not know where it will be, but at least we should learn to recognize the phase that it will be going through! I know you would like to ask me, **"How long will it last?"** The answer stems from the analysis of the cyclical market phases, valid for each type of financial instrument.

Here are the steps!

1-Accumulation, rather moderate and regular growth characterized by rising and relatively high volumes; it is a phase in which the big institutional capital is beginning to move.

2- Bubble, where the market takes a concrete bullish direction and many operators, even small and medium operators, are attracted by the rapid economic returns, rather than by the validity of the technological projects that are behind them. At this stage, the bubble expresses very high volatility, often without any economic motivation. This phase raises the prices and its duration is sanctioned by the emergence of the next phase.

3- Distribution, a short period of further increase or stagnation of the values in which institutional investors begin to lighten their positions selling to occasional investors.

4- Bubble bursting, phase of sudden market collapse, called "panic selling", often linked to spurious motives such as 11[th]September, the crisis of Subprime, etc. This collapse usually returns the market values relatively close to the original values at the beginning of the cycle, to start a new phase of accumulation. The explosion of the speculative bubble is also linked to factors such as:

-The resizing of the optimistic profit prospects of earnings (trust);

-The difficulty of finding new investors willing to buy at a price, which, in the meantime, has become too high;

-The monetization of capital by those who bought previously.

The crypto-assessments, according to my modest point of view, are still in the early stages of the **"speculative bubble"**. Cryptos go up and down, without apparent reasons but many movements are typically institutional, and are proof that they are already on the market from the first stage to earn much more than us, small savers.

We have already said so many times, the investment in crypto is **speculative**, and you have to be able to deal psychologically with the great volatility of this market, especially when it goes against you. **Volatility is cemented into the system**, for some fundamental reasons:

-Most of those who approach crypto, **invest in it randomly**, without analytical and evaluation skills towards the many projects and then there are those who present new currencies;

-**The market is still not overflowing,** i.e. there are too few investors and not much capital being invested, so imagine what could happen, for example, after the 2020 Olympics in Japan, the first crypto-digitalized country since 1stApril 2017. Now the crypto market is "only" worth just over 120 billion Dollars, too small compared to other mega speculative markets like Forex, so you might understand that we are just at the beginning!

-**The number of daily transactions** is still very low, compared to more traditional markets and the BTC requires urgent maintenance to be made faster.

-**The bitcoin graph is mirroring** many actions of the Internet generation (Apple, Microsoft, etc.), so the story repeats itself and will be repeated endlessly.

-**Many currencies will disappear** within a few years and their operators will be like startup supporters or bankruptcy networks that come down into the market only to squeeze capital by deceiving people, so be careful to only invest in the best ones.

The investment in crypto as a reserve of value will be in the hands of those who will buy them at a discount and will have the tenacity to keep them for the long term, **despite the high volatility**.

The real trick is **to identify the new "Amazon"** of the next decade, those crypto with excellent intrinsic values, which you can buy for a few cents and in large quantities, and then splash out hundreds of dollars after some time, for our own opulence and happiness and for all our loved ones!

"Learn to surf on volatility,
as long as the bubble is intact."

CHAPTER 6:
WHAT IS AN I.C.O.?

Another secret that you absolutely have to learn about this six-zero world, is certainly the possibility of participating in an **I. C. O.** (Initial Coin Offering). What is it? It's very simple! Have you ever heard of **I. P. O.** for shares, i.e. new placements on the market? Now, the I. C. O. (hereafter written as ICO) is the fee for crypto-exchange payments. It is a system for online investors to raise new currencies with special features. In 2016, more than two hundred million new currencies were amassed using this method. Knowing how to recognize the best new placements on the market in advance, could bring significant benefits to your portfolio! Some famous examples were the Edgeless and Gnosis issues, which at the opening of the negotiations reached about 500% and 400% respectively.

What is the secret?

The thing that few people know is that before you enter a new currency into the market, you can participate in a pre-auction within a pre-arranged date with a maximum cap of capital to be raised, at a discount price, much lower than the initial quotation price! Now imagine doing such a thing with a selection of the large amount of digital currencies that will be issued, from now on and into the future! I hope you have already done some calculations. This is the dream of every investor: to earn a lot with minimum effort! Maximize your investment!

Where are they?

ICOs are published on one of the industry's most popular forums: **Bitcoin talk**. The project developers present the documents setting out the objectives that the "startup" would like to achieve, together with a whole series of other analytical information that could be useful for investors or their advisors.

Are they always safe?

Absolutely not! The platforms are full of ICOs that have just been listed, which miserably collapse from two BTCs to a few Satoshi. Because of its unregulated nature, they could entail major risks for the reckless investor, degenerating into real fraud. We even know of projects that have failed before they were negotiated. And what happens to the money? Forget about it, because the transactions are not verifiable and there is no governing body. Therefore, open your eyes and never exaggerate.

How can we protect ourselves? There is no established and completely safe way, just common sense! In my experience, a method that guarantees sufficient protection must respond to a famous saying: "You either know how to do it, or you ask"! I mean that if you have acquired the necessary skills to evaluate the offer over time, you also proceed with the analysis of at least these factors:

-A tangible avant-garde project on Blockchain;

-A detailed Business Plan with the relative expertise in the team, so that it can be implemented;

-A sufficiently large potential market;

-Ideal timing for launch.

If you think you are not capable of doing it, then ask! Ask experts who do it for a living, you pay them and they help you earn much more than you paid. Nothing could be easier, saving time and resources, whilst multiplying the investment, excluding costs incurred!

"You either know how to do it, or you ask"!

CHAPTER 7:
HOW TO MANAGE?

A careful portfolio management, whatever its nature, is the gospel for every investor. You cannot expect to make a profit if you don't increase your management skills. This topic has been extensively discussed in our previous book, which I invite you to go and buy! The understanding and application of the passages contained in it could help you greatly on your path of financial and personal growth, which you shouldn't think of completing separately. Let's see how to apply these practical tips concisely and realistically.

-The first step is certainly **to idealize and then put down in writing,** what you would like to accomplish. Never improvise, because you will lose sight of the objectives and work would never go ahead. The basic rule for reducing risk is that the investment is inversely proportional to the hazard of the financial instrument: I will devote more money to investments allow hazard and vice versa, less resources in tools dangerous. A classic global diversification of one's own assets should include a breakdown like this: 40% in bonds, 20% in liquidity, 15% in shares, 10% in real estate, 10% commodities and 5% in speculative instruments including bitcoin and Altcoin. This is the predominant step and for this reason, I will give **a typical example**. Let's start with the only certain data in our possession: how much money do we have? For example, let's say we have a assets of 100,000. We have to allocate 5% of it to speculation with cryptos, for a value equal to 5,000, okay? In the plan I decide to share these 5K in 60% bitcoin and 40% Altcoin, so it would be respectively 3k and 2K.OK?

-Open your first Exchange to Hold, the wallet, such as Blockchain, Coinbase, Bitstamp, etc. to enter the market with 5k when there are ideal conditions for buy (sudden drop in prices). Here you will keep, you will hold your liquidity in BTC that will appreciate over time, thus raising your store of value.

-We witness a steep descent and **decide to trade in BTC** our portion of established assets. We remind you that the future maturities on BTC of the Chicago Mercantile Exchange (CME) have a very negative impact on the Crypto market, excellent maturities if you want to enter the market "at a discount" of up to 15%. For ease of calculation a bitcoin, we paid it 1k. For maximize security, in case of huge capital, I could think about transferring the first three BTC to an offline wallet like the Ledger Nano S or X, or other new types.

-I would also proceed to secure registration in platforms for handling such as the famous **Bittrex or Binance**, for transfer the 3/4 of the initial 40% (equal to 1.5 BTC) from the wallet destined to transform into Altcoin for the "long-term". In addition to bitcoin, select the most valuable projects to invest in in the long term. If my attention will fall on five Altcoins, of course in each I will enter with 1/5 of 1.5 BTC = 0.3 bitcoin.

-If you decide to also want to **undertake the trading**, I would proceed to the transfer of the last quarter of 40% initial (0.5 BTC) in suitable **Binance**-type platforms for coin "pure" or the hugely popular **BitMex** to trade in your risk and danger with leveraged derivatives. In addition, here I would choose an equal distribution in more quality Altcoins, for example, 0.1 bitcoin for five different currencies. Obviously, diversification into several coins reduces the risk of loss if I swapped everything to one Altcoin. The simpler and more profitable rules that I would recommend you follow are the: buy low and sell high; not persist on a single coin in order not to immobilize its counter; do not improvise but plan goals of partial and total entry and exit, and respect them! Any insights will be present in the private channel.

-Always keep in mind that **you have to learn the method**, therefore, do not worry if you move small quantities because if you manage to raise the crypto heritage with them, let alone with big transactions!

-**Set aside part of your cash flow monthly**, exchanging it in BTC to dispose of it at your convenience and in according to your current needs: leave them in bitcoin, exchange them in Altcoin or enlarge your trading account! Remember that, as with all other tools financials, strong falls are an opportunity for accumulation, while very high rises are an opportunity for small ones liquidations, to monetize and diversify again.

-In the following, distribute a minimum percentage of crypto in **Mining** and **Lending** trying to find your personal dimension, without ever exaggerating.

-Earn and manage your crypto carefully in the form of management, through movements based on the **protection** of the same!

Use the strategies shown to multiply enormously your earnings, because the continuous increase in demand, will determine the elevation of the price of the cryptos.

*"Don't have hurry because **patience** is the real key to success"!*

CRYPTOCURRENCIES ON MOBILE APP

In a society of "walking deads" that now favors and defines the personal telephone as the most watched appliance ever, it would be stupid not to assist the reader in using this device effectively and efficiently. First, we advise you to dedicate a page or a folder, only to the Crypto App, to find them all together, without wasting precious time! Remember the three fundamental pillars, now you should do whatever it takes to go along with them at all costs. In fact, for the best possible level of information, I recommend registering in all those channels in which you can draw from professionals, friends and acquaintances who share this same hobby with you. **Telegram**, I think it is the most suitable app for this purpose, making a selection of the best groups, starting with ours. Then I recommend **Polox**, a truly exceptional, always free, very versatile app that allows you to view the price of the major crypto-currencies, in different platforms, against different Fiat currencies, the most purchased, the most sold, in alphabetical order and much more. Another indispensable app is **CoinMarketCap**, in which you can analyse in depth what could be your next Altcoins, in addition to the market capitalization. The app, which will allow security on two levels (2fa) in, will also be fundamental many platforms of all kinds, **Google Authenticator**. After registration and really simple setting, it will generate a timed six-digit code, which you must promptly enter on request on the platforms of which you have already downloaded the app (**Blockchain**, **Bittrex**, **Bitstamp**, **Coinbase**, **Binance**, **BitMex**, etc.) for use even on the move. Then, I would download an important App, **BitcoinMap**, which would allow me to verify the local development of all those activities of goods and services that accept bitcoins also partially for your purchases and ATM on the territory.

If you want to operate at a higher level, I would recommend you Apps like **TabTrader** for the very important alerts, alarms service, thanks to which we will not have to be constantly connected to check the price levels but we can set them a priori on any coin and be notified selectively with a notification of your choice, to then operate what we have set at the operational level. Continuing, I believe you cannot do without **Blockfolio** because it is a virtual wallet that allows you to add all your purchases, or all the coins that you are following closely, in special watch list managed easily with alerts to change their consistency, at your convenience. Finally, I would recommend using **Bitcoin Ticker Widget**, which really allows a great series of possibilities with the charts and with the values of the major crypto.

We learn to use the smartphone as a tool that works for us, enslaved to our needs and not only to waste precious time!

"The phone is a smartphone

not a foolphone"!

HOW TO WITHDRAW REAL MONEY

The withdrawal of real money after changing the cryptos is perceived by people as a real dilemma. At the moment, I have no intention of withdrawing money, because it would be stupid to think of withdrawing my investment in something that was doing so well, subtracting a reserve of value that is being used more and more every day. Do you not think so? I'm going to tell you more, I had thought about selling this book in BTC, but I immediately realized that the Italians are not ready for this step, so I am just informing you of the possibilities. In the near future, I certainly think it will be good to pay for future services in crypto.

I advise you to support the investment in crypto, with an amount that you have made and that you do not need immediately, otherwise I don't really think it is worth it!

Every day we see news in the industry, and technology combined with competition will bring significant changes in the coming years, in favor of customer demand!

Each of us has different needs and if you have to change bitcoin to Euro, you will do so for two possible needs: to withdraw it or to spend it. I assure you that you can do this with different systems.

HOW TO WITHDRAW BITCOINS

The most common and popular system is offered directly by specialized companies or Wallets Online such as **Bitstamp**, **Spectrocoin**, **Criptopay** or **Xapo**. You may require the use of a rechargeable card costing about $10, which is delivered to your home, on which you can safely transfer your bitcoins to make purchases or withdraw Euros at any ATM in the world. The card is ideal for withdrawals of up to a few hundred Euros, but if they are larger, I recommend that you use a bureau de change so that you only pay   the commission required for the brokerage once.

Less common, and present in a few corners of Italy, are ATMs (Automated Teller Machine), usually orange in color with the symbol of the BTC currency, thanks to which it is possible to withdraw or instantaneously move cash from or to your wallet, converted according to the exchange rate in force at the time of the transaction. The operation is similar to transactions carried out in person, because it requires the App wallet uploaded onto your smartphone, capable of generating the address (if you send) or the QR Code (if you receive), to be applied to the optical reader to carry out security checks.

Another possibility of changing bitcoins into Euros is given by the crypto trading in **exchange for cash**, through people who live near your city, still using the same simple App such as Blockchain, for the transaction. This method can be considered to reduce transaction costs between different wallets. Please note that you will need to take your "bank" with you on your mobile phone, App and you may be subject to robbery or scams if you don't keep your eyes open. It is sufficient to match the request with the offer and the exchange can take place. If you don't have these social skills, you can use sites such as **localbitcoins.com** with caution, thanks to which you can exchange with anonymous people with feedback or people close to you and you can buy or sell at competitive prices, below market prices by a few percentage points. Another thing to try!

"Pick up now is stupid,

let your investment run, run, run "!

HOW CAN YOU SPEND BITCOINS?

As you have seen so far, an App, address or QR Code is enough to make an easy transaction using the bitcoins in your wallet. On the network there is a myriad of sites and services that accept bitcoins as a form of payment. The list is constantly increasing, and you can already buy everything from electronics to trips, from watches to jewels and so on. To understand further that bitcoins are becoming more commonplace in everyday life, and that in a certain sense, they are trying to reach out to the real world and no longer remain only digital, I recommend you visit the site **coin map**. It highlights the local map of shops, professionals, hotels and services that accept bitcoins as a form of payment.

Only by seeing with their own eyes and touching it with their own hands, as St. Thomas did, can people move away from the skepticism that surrounds crypto? Relying on people from whom you already buy, who you trust and consider competent and reliable, you can vary the aura of suspicion that severely limits popular trust, giving new impetus to crypto, until the final consecration.

"Bitcoins are all around us! ".

CHAPTER 8:
LIMITS AND TRENDS

We have already discussed many topics and to tell the truth I think you have already created in your mind a fairly defined image of what the bitcoin phenomenon is. We are now close to the end of this work and I would begin to draw the first conclusions, weighing the opposite sides of a coin, the front of which looks like a real unstoppable Superstar towards climbing in world hits, while the rear part, the less visible one, highlights controversial aspects, often dictated by ignorance on the subject, which I will try to stem.

In fact, from my small and univocal point of view, I declare that to eliminate most of the problems of society, the main road is that of contrasting ignorance, personal presumption without skills to granting quality information to then convey the person in specific training. Do you think its utopia? Ignoring does not simply mean "not knowing" but there are dangerous partnerships that you will have to remember:

-Ignorance and freedom lead to chaos;

-Ignorance and poverty lead to crime;

-Ignorance and power lead to tyranny;

-Ignorance and religion lead to terrorism;

-Ignorance and social networks lead to diffusion;

-Ignorance and money lead to corruption.

For this reason, the fight against "not knowing" must be a priority for everyone, especially for those who have the burden of educating other people such as family, school, governments, coaches, etc. Returning to us, in this chapter we will examine the limits of crypto and the future trends to which they are projected.

"Often the limits are not what we think but only the fruit of our fears"!

WHAT ARE THE LIMITS OF CRYPTOS?

They are very few if weighed up against the virtues. Let's see the most relevant.

Internal Contrasts

The only real obstacle to growth came from the internal disagreements between designers and maintenance miners of Blockchain, who wanted to make their own thinking prevail at the expense of others. The tensions arise from the well-known **"Hong Kong agreement"**, signed by representatives of each of the two categories and then reneged by other factions, for the SegWit protocols, which became SegWit2x. After a new meeting, it was thought that a compromise had been found, known as the "New York Accord". The result: tensions continue to exist and it even resulted in a split into two Blockchain: BTC and BCC/BCH (**bitcoincash**) on 1 August 2017. The crypto boom has certainly been facilitated by the capabilities of all parties, and so far, it has truly rewarded anyone and everyone, notwithstanding the opposing interests. I think it would be really stupid to jeopardize the possibility of changing the world, by letting personal interests get in the way, something which is far from the BTC philosophy.

Usability

It is defined as the degree of ease and satisfaction with which the interaction between man and an instrument takes place, which in this case is the BTC and the other cryptocurrencies. Mindful of the notions learned, do you think they are difficult to use? As usual, it's all the fault of the total misinformation of the average reader. In fact, much of the popular doubt from the fact that it is believed that these currencies cannot have a global adoption, because they cannot be physically probed, it is believed that they cannot be spent and that it is not as practical as the national currency! Do you personally handle Fiat cash? I very little and it will be less and less, because the governments, in this way, would like to eliminate the escaped, the undeclared. The global mass adoption will lead the crypto to increasingly assert themselves and be respected by anyone. Do you know that you could be among the first to innovate an old-fashioned system like the financial one, reasoning like the first, those who will be the greatest, and not like the last? The history of finance teaches it with several examples. I just ask you to put aside what you can and think like the thousands of new rich people who have acted in this way, buying and keeping in the wallets the valuable shares of Colossi such as Boeing, Microsoft, Amazon, etc.

Quality Dilution

A curious phenomenon is that of companies that, to ride the crypto bubble to the fullest, are moving away from bitcoin to always issue new coins or build different platforms. The market respects only one King, bitcoin with its Dominance over the entire market, of over 67% (end of 2019), all the remaining initiatives will only bring capital within the system but I don't know how many will survive. Currencies are multiplying visibly, scams as well but the court will remain restricted to a few large competitors. Many think that bitcoin is already divided, that many people don't use it because they don't know where and how to do it! I ask you a question: would you ever spend a secondary currency that could be appreciated indefinitely, when you can choose to continue using the primary? Of course not! Then remember to **invest in quality**, because if you had to make a blunder, you would not reinvest in other crypto-currencies, trust me! Only by keeping the best crypto in your wallets, you will set aside a nice reserve of benefit to your "conventional" heritage, to add to your starvation pension, when you decide to retire!

Coin Hacker attacks

Crypto-evaluations are capitalizing on the interest of everyone and especially of those who would like to earn money. We don't know if the numerous news reports on hacking, i.e. illegal penetrations into accounts to subtract what does not belong to them, is the result of truth or fantasy, but one thing is certain: the values in the field are so high that it would be obvious to expect cyber attacks. They could be by competitors of different currencies trying to discredit other people's protocols, but also by governments to undermine the reliability of cryptos, etc. From whichever part the attack arrives, it makes sense to not use only one Wallet/Exchanger service, thus diversifying the risk of illegal entry.

Finally, this problem would be completely ruled out if you were to adopt a multi-level identification security, the use of pin codes for withdrawals and Wallets which can be used offline such as Electrum (software) or Ledger Nano (hardware key).

Bitcoin future

How much media hype has aroused the birth of this future of the Chicago Mercantile Exchange (CME). In my experience, when a business is in the newspapers, it is already time to stay away from it! By the time we write this edition of the book,

Bitcoin is already ten years old and having invested in the early days, it would have represented a colossal accumulation of money. The masses discovered Bitcoin by a large majority with the launch of future thinking that it was no longer a bubble but an investment opportunity! The first big real difference is given by the fact that in the past the price of Bitcoin was attributed thanks to the trend of supply and demand; with future, on the other hand, the price of an asset such as a currency, hedge Funds, E.T.F., mutual funds, are generated by mere bets on the price of the same asset, at a certain monthly expiration. To win these bets, financial and banking institutions, both institutional and non-institutional, are ready to put on the market wagons of money to buy or sell them, causing a real imbalance in the natural demand for digital currencies. Now I hope you will understand better why they call these organizations, "big market sharks" because they have no ethics, there is no one behind their White collars but they are only there for profit. Those who speak of Bitcoin as a Ponzi scheme probably don't know how a future works. Since they are on the market, the bitcoin chart seems to have gone mad especially in conjunction with the future deadlines of the end of the month. We agree that the old rule of finance, that is, who has more money to put on the market has the scepter of power but this is like being on a roller coaster ride, with much more nervous movements than in the past, raising its speculative perception more . I would like to say that this was an obligatory passage for cryptocurrencies as has happened for other instruments such as Commodities. The effects of future are highly perceived in the crypto world, due to the usual big problem: large quantities of bitcoins are managed by a very small number of people who could easily agree between them.

Don't worry because the nervous effect will tend to soothe, to decrease, when the Bitcoin quantities are fragmented on larger holders. As long as the future are few, they will only contribute to raising bitcoin's reputation but when they are many more, they will tend to move much more capital on the market and it will be very risky to remain in the position! In fact, the moment that I call appropriate to leave the crypto market will be when future create a real regulated market! To stem this big problem, a great solution is needed: to increase the number of competitors in real tools such as the coveted E.T.F. that, at the moment, the US SEC does not want to take off, despite hundreds of requests received.

Finally, I still remind you that the CME future deadlines on BTC are excellent maturities if you want to enter the market "at a discount" even by 15%.

WHAT ARE THE NEXT TRENDS?

I will repeat it until the evidence contradicts me: crypto-currencies are currently at high risk! As repeated several times, they should be assimilated to a speculative investment, like any other such as forex, binary options, etc. By now, even the transactions carried out through online banks are almost all digital, therefore, the crypto-currencies are not as far from the common ideology, as one might believe. Many suppose that it is a great battle between an old and a new system, but I believe that it is not like that at all, because it is only the normal evolution of things. The systems will coexist, and in the long run one of the two could take over and only the world's populations will decide which side to stay on. Change is now inherent in us, but many don't even notice it. We passed from the urban phone to the smartphone, from purchases to the neighborhood market to the Online, from the PC to the Ipad, from petrol cars to electric cars in a few years. I don't see why not being able to switch to a new financial model, completely self-managed and without burdensome intermediation. Also for these reasons, one of the biggest dangers that could slow down the development of Bitcoin is the continuous frontal attack from the world Central Banks, even if the opinions are completely divergent, among them. The financial world is dominated by the "Debt System" in which the CBs, which I remind you of being private bodies controlled by banks, broker waste paper loans to governments together with an interest rate. We have already talked about it and the banking system is a champion of ambiguity because it is fought by the fact that on the one hand it is becoming aware of its uselessness towards Retail (end customer), while on the other we are extremely certain that rivers of capital of the same banks have financed the same construction of the Blockchain structure and that profit great within the bitcoin charts, obtaining returns that currently no other asset can guarantee anymore. I think global skepticism arises from the nature of the fundamental characteristic of crypto:

Decentralization, which is diametrically opposed to the concept of "Central" Bank!

Furthermore, American monetary policy assimilates crypto-currencies to a potential, a large competitor of the dollar on a global level. The only solution for Americans, the only way forward is to promote a **"Centralized"** crypto market to keep under control the huge flow of capital attracted by its known current and presumably near returns. In my opinion, it is utopia; it is unachievable, even if the current events are full of upheavals and in every field. We do not know what will await us in the next future, but among the possible scenarios, there could also be direct attacks on the Bitcoin protocol, by the Governments controlled by the BC themselves. The latter is studying in-depth the evolution of crypto-currencies, to know how to use them further. The ECB in 2019 bypassed attention on the crypto world by publicly declaring total indifference towards an "insignificant" phenomenon of a few billion dollars (100 at the time), even if the change of Mario Draghi at the helm of the Institute in favor of Lagarde (Ex IMF) has given significant positive impetus to the treatment of matter in an expansionist sense.

The USA, as already said, is the usual paradox because they are now masters in imposing themselves on the world according to the philosophy of "Dividi et Impera" (Philip II of Macedonia), that is, through the subtle and enigmatic sowing to foment total chaos among other peoples to benefit firsthand! The FED has repeatedly stated that the possibility of using a digital currency is not being evaluated, but they are the first to have found a research and control body of the phenomenon, within the IRS, the tax collection agency that represents a section of the National Treasury Department. Ask yourself a question: where are the exchange platforms located among the largest in the world (Coinbase, Bittrex, Kraken, etc.), guess what? Great!

In the States; long lives consistency! But it is not over because the US strategy plans to eradicate any attempt to create alternative markets. But why?

Why do they fear digital currencies so much, in addition to the reasons already stated? The answer requires reasoning!

To understand the following, it will be appropriate to introduce some concepts of macroeconomics. We will begin by making a distinction between traditional economies and modern economies. In the first case, the economy was supported by productivity, thanks to which the average value of the currency always remained the same due to the elimination of inflation and deflation.

In modern economies, however, supported as we know by the public debt and by the CBs that print paper with no value and without underlying, the balance needle is guaranteed by a slight inflation at 2% through which you can play with the rate of interest to bring the currency into stability in the event of a recession.

All over the world, therefore, it is no longer the productivity that balances the economies, despite the BC constantly stimulating sectors and institutional reforms. It's a resounding fake, everyone knows how it works and everyone is fine with it. This type of monetary policy is accepted everywhere. That 2% inflation may seem like a small thing, an acceptable value in the short term. In the long term, if you really want to know, for example at thirty, it determines a cut in **purchasing power** to about 50% of the currency. If absurdly we talked about 3% per year in thirty years this reduction would be about 90% if not more. In fact, American citizens do not realize the loss of purchasing power of their currency because they live in a debt-based system where two thirds of the population have a current account not exceeding $ 5000, currently uses the credit card that moves away from reality and prudent management of its budget. Do you know when Americans ask themselves the first questions? When they travel to other States and compare prices to feed, have fun, etc. far below their own! This constant loss of purchasing power of the dollar makes it increasingly difficult for the Federal Reserve to continue printing currency worthless for the survival of the nation, thus only widening the debt hole to the next point of no return! People are not stupid and these things begin to understand them, to somatize them, resulting in real national discontent as in the rest of the world that result in global protest votes as happened for "Brexit", as happened to the Governments of different European countries, as happened for Trump! Moreover, how will the next be? In this climate of general habituation, however, people begin to experience the existence of a digital currency without inflation that even raises its value at a dizzying rate: bitcoin. Digital currencies in general make us understand the deception perpetrated against us, in which we are first actors. The CB aim to keep the debt system of national currencies upright but, in my opinion, they would do well to think how to go hand in hand and not to oppose them, because as the greatest economists in the world say: the Blockchain and the Bitcoin protocol are only evolution, they can't stop! They are like the internet, the greatest awakening phenomenon of the masses; many have tried to stop him but no one has ever succeeded!

In the rest of the world, the situation is very different. A great example is Japan, a huge world economy, which has given total and unconditional trust to the crypto-currencies because this sentiment is the real fuel of finance. The whole of the East can only trade with Japan in bitcoin, and now, it is a commercial boom. A real trick! Everyone will line up when the Japanese annual results compare and follow suit. First, the smaller economies are looking for redemption, and then the larger ones that will arrive late. The financial outlook will be completely redesigned and not having cryptocurrencies in the wallet will have been the way of today. Bitcoin and a few other digital currencies may be the only ones capable of limiting Fiat's hegemony on a global level. Let's not forget that bitcoin was born only a few years ago and has already claimed to revolutionize the currency markets. It is an ever-expanding ecosystem and is being made increasingly efficient to satisfy a larger number of small investors. Imagine what will happen within a few years, when the embryo will emit the colorful butterfly, when many projects on site will be implemented, such as:

-The number of transactions in BTC will go from 400,000 per day as an hour to the same quantities, per hour with the new **Lightning Network** protocol;

-In some States, wages will be regulated, optionally, also in crypto, totally or partially, as already happens!

-Birth and empowerment of ever new payment processors, with guarantees such as Circle, Baakt, which will regulate exchanges only in cryptocurrencies;

-Daily e-Commerce transactions and commercial databases will be regulated in Blockchain;

-The creation of a product or commercial "sector crypto", for lawyers only, for entrepreneurs, doctors, designs, etc.

-Hedge funds will begin to diversify, trading crypto;

-The gold reserves will continue to be liquidated in favor of cryptocurrencies, assimilated as a new asset of safe haven, together with 10,000 other ongoing projects!

The real Bullish will be the Chinese

We have already seen the importance of the real economy on bitcoin compared to the virtual one induced by artifacts such as debt, future, etc. ... For this reason it is important to analyze the fundamentals of the most active governments in the cryptocurrency transaction: China-Japan E Asia in general. We have already spoken about the Japanese. We will focus now on China. The last year (2019) was a historic year for the Chinese because the gross domestic product closed "only" with a +6% which for a western country would seem a lot but for China, it is the worst since 1992 and they were now thirty years that did not slow down its growth. In addition to the future, I also framed the drop in bitcoin in the reduced spending power of the Chinese and the increase in live speculation. That is, by circulating less money you invest less in high-risk products. However, be careful, the Chinese slowdown could only be a pause for reflection because in countries with strong expansionary economic vocation such as China, it could only be a year of adjustment to reorganize their skills and then return to run much faster towards a bright future. The government does not carry out bailouts for a philosophy based on "natural selection": you will have to do it alone because only then will you learn to become more robust! China is a large productive country that many point to as a voice actor, a counterfeiter of the goods and services of others. It is only envied because today's China is not that of twenty years ago, it is a country that has evolved tremendously and frightens everyone, including the USA. Intelligence is to take an example from your surroundings and improve it! A case in point was generated by the opening of Baakt, a platform with which the New York Stock Exchange will list futures with underlying assets for the first time, linked to a real deposit and custody in bitcoin. China immediately sensed the big futuristic business and "stimulated" several institutional investors to open a company based in Hong Kong: **CoinFlex**. Well, why wasn't it done in the EU too? Because it is bigoted, it is old and does not innovate; do you know what happens to those who do not modernize? Finally, the Chinese Central Bank encourages the local banking system to avoid the stagnation of the internal economy. Like? It came out in all the financial newspapers! The People's Bank of China will use funds of almost 115 billion dollars to start expansionist moves that will not go in the direction of crypto-currencies as well. So, the Chinese prospects are much more than rosy for the coming months and years ahead of the European sclerotic bandwagon.

The mother wave has yet to arrive

Well yes, the biggest wave is expected by everyone. Obviously, there will be those who surfer it and those who are overwhelmed by it. A fairly shared forecast will be the significant overcoming of the twenty thousand dollars of the last historical maximum and many ask: When will it happen? The answer is relatively simple: When the crypto market and bitcoins in the first place, will now be perceived as a certainty and only from it will total trust in this type of investment be born. Anyone will want to appropriate bitcoin fractions but it will already be on the moon and many will repeat to themselves: they had told me so many times! If you have understood the teachings of this work, I explained how to ride the bitcoin opportunity and, by far, the most profitable over time is to position yourself on the market during a Panic Selling, one of the frequent massive sales of digital currency. One of my most famous quotes is: If you want to get rich, you have to buy when others have their hands in their hair! This must be followed by a monthly provision commensurate with your abilities, until the great sidereal launch awaited by all takes place. On its own, this simplistic method will guarantee you crazy ROIs.

At the moment, I do not see other great possibilities because for the real estate market you will have to invest heavily and it is in the gold market, I could only get rich if extreme conditions occurred.

Another term that many people don't know about in finance is: **patience**! If you position yourself on the crypto market with the necessary patience, you could also find yourself with a hundredfold investment in a few years. You do not believe me, do you? I just hope that at the time of reading this last chapter, ETFs have already been admitted to trading! I foresee big fireworks. This means thousands of bankers and white-collar workers around the world who will receive a letter of dismissal from their institutions.

With the above, the continuous news of new adoptions of the Blockchain and Bitcoin protocol, together with the typical and peculiar "scarcity effect" of the true Superstar of the crypto market, its price could probably go up a lot and surely we will be able to witness it and tell our children to have taken part, as protagonists, in the greatest financial revolution of all time!

"Bitcoin is projected up there,
where you could never imagine it could reach! ".

CONCLUSIONS

I hope that my efforts to make this work worthy of your attention have been rewarded. As we have seen throughout the chapters, according to my modest point of view, crypto-exchange rates are the best way to go both in terms of high yield and privacy reserve, so I believe that today they are the instrument of choice to protect your money from deflation and inflation and to unthinkably raise your reserve of value set aside to protect you for the future.

To best sum up my thoughts, I feel I have to give you some typical advice as the **"good father of the family"** would. I recognize the responsibility and it is therefore, obvious that I must give you some straightforward information about the use of this fantastic instrument, drawing your attention to the possible risks due to the usual problems that afflict mankind: greed, haste, fickleness, superficiality, parasitism and the desire to remain in absolute ignorance!

Unfortunately, you'll find many sources of information around from people that maybe don't even hold crypto in their wallet and maybe don't know the difference between a wallet and a trading platform. This is the first problem. As I always say, the investment with the best interest rate is: **effective information**! In this period, information is very limited and does not contribute to a worthy awareness of the benefits of this revolution. The idea of this book was conceived to counteract the incorrect use of information that many people have adopted for their own benefit, the ignorance of the uninvolved.

For these reasons, in order not to succumb to this selective market prematurely, I would like to leave you with a list of general guidelines that you will have to follow to implement your financial skills, because I would be really happy to be able to leave you with some valuable information, so that you can continue to expand your personal skills.

Never lose

My first finance rule is taken from Warren Buffett. Is there or is there not a reason why he is the wealthiest investor on the planet? Secondly, I advise you to re-read the first rule to keep in mind the importance of this passage. The protection of your assets is a priority over the ability to make a profit. You must protect yourself so that you can continue to operate. Never diminish the efficiency of your money. The big difference is that if you leave money that you have not invested in your traditional bank account, you will see it eroded by inflation and bank charges. If you put a small portion of it into a wallet and change it into BTC, you won't have these problems and you run the serious risk of seeing them increase tenfold in a few years.

Diversify

Diversification is essential to protect your capital. At present, there are at least eight hundred crypto-evaluations, and it is very difficult to discriminate between the good ones and those which will not see the light of the New Year. You'll be wondering: Where can I get accurate information on where to place my money? First of all, I will come to your aid, allowing you to enter a private channel of mine on Telegram, referred to at the end of the book, so that we can get to know each other personally and be able to continue with a dialogue. The best advice is to invest in quality, because it is always rewarding!

Do not take risks

Aggressive tools like crypto, because of their risk intrinsic, they could allow more earnings, but also many more losses. For this reason, the big risk you have to attribute a small wallet. Generally, I recommend convert **no more than 5%** of your capital into crypto-currencies. The investment must always be reversed proportional to its riskiness. Other investments, according to a reasoned breakdown, they will affect the more solid pillars and with less surprises, which are the Bonds, the Shares, Real Estate and Commodities (raw materials). I remind you that the medium to long term results of yours portfolios will be the result of the set of tools and not the individuals who make it up! All the Gurus of the finance, I say all, show that knowing how to invest in adequate financial instruments, do not derive from improvisation, but from appropriate knowledge obsessive of the same and from a more important management of personal emotion. To never risk, reinvest part of the first earnings in training to always learn new things to get there first and better than the others!

Plan

Do it by writing, setting yourself achievable goals. Paper and pen in hand, write down the rules on the corner of a clean sheet of A3 paper and begin to use them in writing a possible draft of a financial plan. If the plan is in your mind, but not on paper, you'll never get round to doing anything!

Successful Trading

Those who survive enough in the market to become successful Traders (5% of the total) are not only experts in trading methodologies and disciplined users of these systems, but are also scholars of their own personality and the risks associated with their techniques. Frankly, one cannot imagine an improvement in one's own finances without greater awareness of one's own personal abilities. Growth must go hand in hand, in all skills, expanding them every day. You will not only be a well-off, but above all a man best for the people around you!

Do not trust anyone

Many of those you will meet on your way will be experts in currency encryption. Personally, I have written a book about it, but I think I have only explored the tip of the iceberg. Who is the only person you can trust? Only yourself! Try to constantly increase your knowledge in the field and everything will become clearer! My advice is simple and is based on experience; I would not want you to make the mistakes I have made in the past. Let's see some:

-A common mistake is to keep for too long time an Altcoin in Wallets, because it will be issued on market a new currency with improved protocol, for reset the value of yours, so I recommend getting some good returns, sell totally or partially, capitalize and then move on to another project Never use a single platform, hackers punish those who do not know how to protect themselves with wallets.

- Never use a single platform; the hackers they punish hardly the unwary who don't know how to protect yourself with Wallets.
-Do not convert your bitcoins into Fiat currency, because you would reduce the store of value and make yours visible movements. We have the systems to avoid the problem treated, you have no more excuses!

It is often said that whoever is there will see! I add that whoever enters it methodically, will enjoy it, in the face of those who will not and will remain uninformed spectator! This is really a book that I would have had the pleasure of reading years ago and I am sure that today I would live in the Cayman Islands (smile!). You too could have some great satisfactions, but if you are not willing to follow my advice, then leave it alone and look for a traditional job where you spend 8-10 hours of your time, for a starvation salary!

I have always wanted to try to change the mentality of the **"average reader"**, offering him a new view. There is a new perspective in this book futuristic but current, in which everyone becomes the bank of himself, everyone manages their own money without intermediaries, and it becomes the real added value. Neither will you be able?
I did my best, now it's your turn!

MY INTERVIEW
"THE FUTURE OF CRYPTOS"!

This is an interview I gave for a famous online newspaper below. Given the result, I cannot help but give knowledge to my readers too! Here it is, in full!

Tell us a little about yourself and how you got closer to the world of Bitcoin / cryptocurrencies.
Hi, I define myself as a self-publisher, prudent investor and "serial producer of passive income" because it is now twenty years that, thanks to my inexhaustible curiosity and my unstoppable desire for continuous personal growth, I have understood prematurely that the most important thing about great Businessman and that trends must be anticipated to ride them fully.

It is necessary to reason, as I often write in my channels, in an opposite way to the masses: buy an underlying (obviously after analysis) when others disown it or are selling it massively and contrarily, sell when "the business is in the newspapers", that is when all the others also buy at very high prices. In my works, of which many Amazon Bestsellers, I have tried to produce something that I missed after my studies, tools not only for reflection but with precise step by step that could help the reader, looking for his own personal realization .

Specifically for cryptocurrencies, I approached already in 2015 and in 2016, I started buying and accumulating bitcoins and Altcoins, always keeping in mind that these are speculative instruments to which to allocate a maximum of 5% of their investment portfolios.

The genesis of the book: why you thought it necessary to share your views.

I created the book because of the great proliferation of Scam business (pyramidal and Ponzi schemes) which also affected many of my friends. It was necessary to clarify and I know only one system: effective information, which I believe to be the investment with the highest interest rate.

Today this need is even more felt because of the internet that I assimilate to a huge ocean of information, often useless and misleading for the reader looking for a destination, on his slender raft! The book (as you have seen) is not only informative, but it explains what better ways are to buy cryptocurrencies and the future scenarios that are already emerging. Then, an after-sales service that sees my readers pass through a totally free private channel to ask anything from a dedicated community, frankly I think not many people will grant it.

What do you think of the current state of health of cryptocurrencies and the underlying technology?

The cryptocurrencies are in excellent health! What ordinary people have not completely learned and that the success of digital coins is due precisely to the concept of the technology that supports them: the Blockchain! This is the real genius, an encrypted database and, at the same time public in respect of privacy, it would make every institution, financial organization, etc. happy. For this reason the success of cryptocurrencies and equal to that of the web is unstoppable, it is simply the future!

Adoption (a term widely used in this area) is at impressive levels and increases every year: cryptocurrencies are a necessary consequence of the current economy.

What are the forecasts for the near future, that is, how do you imagine cryptocurrencies in the coming years?

My forecasts are entirely positive; otherwise I wouldn't have bought them (smile)! Seriously, I will briefly explain the reasons for my optimism. 2020 will be the year of the consecration of the crypto and species of the **"superstar"** bitcoin (with its 67% of Dominance in the digital market) due to the new Lightning Network protocol, the Halving and the Olympic games that will be held in the first country that gave bitcoin a "legal tender" with a law of 01.04.2017: the great Japan! Imagine that anyone can pay with the most popular crypto, any good and service due to the parallelism of local currency, the Yen, and bitcoin. A worldwide showcase in which millions of people will physically approach the future, a virtual approach, just what the crypto felt the need to have. Other states are doing the same thing: bomb news of a few days ago that France will be the first European nation to equip itself with a digital currency, thanks perhaps to the new president of the ECB, Lagarde, also French! Furthermore, a great technician, the former Italian finance minister, Tremonti, has publicly confirmed that the phenomenon is simply the future and that it is frankly unstoppable. The whole planet is waiting for ETFs on bitcoins to explode in a titanic way, as happened for gold! Finally, in a globalized world that has made popular protest a real custom; would you still imagine banks that broker our money? Absolutely not! The bitcoin motto is **"Be your own bank"**, be the bank of yourself, without intermediaries, the

banking and financial world has already understood this but it is too late!
Are you ready for the digital revolution?

"I look forward to seeing you on my portal for lots of free content"!

AFTER SALES RESOURCES

We are now at the end of my efforts and know that your opinion is important to me! Knowing if I did a good job or how I could improve would help me grow, therefore, I would be really grateful if you made a conscientious review on Amazon or on my personal website. For this gesture, I would reward you by allowing you to enter our private Telegram channel! I would also invite you to subscribe to one of my new channels to continue the experience together, to be informed about any news and to collaborate on major projects for the future!

Our global portal
www.tonylocorriere.org

Private group on Telegram
Conscientiously review the book, contact me privately, send me a screenshot to gain access to the group where you can ask me anything.

Public page on Facebook

@bitcoinsuperstar

One of the few on the web to issue weekly free bitcoin and crypto reports every Saturday morning.

Search for my name on Amazon

For previous publications or reviews.

Search for my name on Linkedin

For more information about me!

Finally, I really congratulate you for having finished reading this book! I toast to your success now by wishing you a good life and ... **"Work Hard"**, because without hard work, you will never have anything!

Tony LOCORRIERE

Until next publication! Good life...

END